PSYCHIC
ANIMALS

PSYCHIC ANIMALS

Superstition, Science, and Extraordinary Tales

Michelle Waitzman

ARCTURUS

Picture Credits

Getty Images: 40 (*Harry Todd*), 63 (*Rick Madonik*),
81 (*Dibyangshu Sarkar*), 93 (*Rodney Brindamour*),
108 (*Roland Weihrauch*), 111 (*STR / Stringer*), 113 (*Alex Wong*)

Shutterstock: 6, 9, 11, 16, 19, 23, 25, 28, 31, 34, 38, 45, 50, 53,
57, 59, 60, 69, 74, 76, 84, 86, 89, 94, 95, 96, 99, 103, 104, 114

Provided by author: 13 (*Wyse Photography*),
36 (*Janelle Mackie/NZ USAR Search Dog Association*),
47 (*Anne de Haas Photography*), 55 (*Michelle Waitzman*),
71 (*Bryan March*), 83 (*Hollie Devlin*)

Wikimedia Commons: 32 (*Ministry of Information UK*),
49 (*Cpl. Jennifer Pirante*), 106 (*Sotheby's New York*)

ARCTURUS

This edition published in 2017 by Arcturus Publishing Limited
26/27 Bickels Yard, 151–153 Bermondsey Street,
London SE1 3HA

ISBN: 978-1-78428-673-6
AD005630UK

Printed in China

CONTENTS

INTRODUCTION

Animals never ceases to amaze us with the funny, clever and sometimes downright mysterious things they do, from animals that like to surf or pets that travel seemingly impossible distances to find their owners, to creatures that bring up abandoned animals of other species and dogs that risk their lives to save humans they don't even know. These stories are usually presented in the news as light-hearted breaks from the more serious items, but some animal stories have scientific implications, like the discovery that dogs can identify dangerous blood-sugar levels in their diabetic owners or even smell cancer on the breath.

As scientists delve deeper, some myths appear 'busted' while others continue to confound us. This book will introduce you to many of the riddles and miracles of animal science. You may well be shocked by the incredible skills and fascinating genetic adaptations in the animals you see around you. From the majestic horse and the loyal dog that have served us well for centuries, to the humble dung beetle, the animal kingdom is full of surprises.

ANCIENT TALES

Our belief that animals are more than they first appear, potentially even possessing supernatural powers, dates back to some of the oldest cultures on Earth. One example is the Aboriginal culture in Australia, which began between 40,000 and 60,000 years ago. The Aboriginal creation myth is called 'The Dreaming', and in many parts of Australia it features a creature called the Rainbow Serpent. In some versions of the story, this magical animal lived under the earth and held all the world's creatures in her belly. When she emerged on the surface, she created all the features of the land and released the newly born animals into the world. If that isn't impressive enough, she is also credited with creating the sun, fire and all the colours of the world.

The ancient Egyptians associated animals with their gods. In fact, most of their gods either had animal forms or had the body of a human and the head of an animal. For this reason, the Egyptians would consider certain animals to be sacred and protect them. Their most sacred animal was the cat. Both the great sun god Ra and the goddess Bastet (who started out as a war goddess but transmuted into a protective goddess of the home) were depicted as cats, and cats were kept as pets and held in high esteem in the households of ancient Egypt. They were so well protected that killing a cat, even accidentally, was punishable by death. They were also one of the few animals to be mummified. Cats were thought to help with fertility because they were so nurturing of their own young, and pregnant women would wear amulets of the cat goddess Bastet with kittens to protect their unborn children.

SEEING THE FUTURE

One of the most frequent supernatural abilities people have attached to animals is the ability to predict the future. While many of the old superstitions have died out, some are still around and new ones are constantly coming to light. For example, later in the book we will look at the belief that animals can predict natural disasters, such as earthquakes. This belief has been around for thousands of years, but we continue to investigate the science that lies behind the superstitions. We'll also examine the more recent phenomenon of people looking to animals to predict the outcome of sporting events. While this

'talent' must be taken with several grains of salt, people seem to find it irresistible.

Today we may treat the idea of fortune-telling animals with a healthy degree of scepticism, but in the past people took it very seriously, often to the detriment of the animal. The Etruscans, who lived in an area north of Rome between the 8th and 3rd centuries BC, were one of the first people we know of to practice 'haruspication'. This involved the rather gruesome practice of sacrificing an animal and laying out its entrails, then interpreting the results to predict the future. Even earlier, the Babylonians did a similar thing with sheep's

Cats were revered and considered very sacred in Ancient Egypt. Killing a cat was punishable by death.

livers. The Romans became huge believers in the ability to read the future in an animal's innards, and the famous warning to Julius Caesar to 'beware the Ides of March' was supposedly made by a haruspex (entrails reader). Although the practice became less popular in the 4th and 5th centuries, toward the later days of Rome, it continued into the Middle Ages in parts of Europe.

In many cultures, seeing an animal in a particular place, or behaving in a certain way, was interpreted as an omen. For example, a black cat crossing your path has been considered bad luck in many European cultures for centuries, while a cat sneezing was said to predict rain. In Medieval Europe, a bat, robin or pigeon flying into your house was bad luck, as was seeing an owl during the day. But other creatures were more welcome; seeing a white or brown mouse or a hedgehog was said to bring good luck, and a squirrel was a sign of happiness to come.

A FAMILIAR STORY

Beginning in the 15th century, the practice of witchcraft, real or imagined, was targeted by religious leaders across Europe and eventually in the United States. One of the superstitions associated with witches was the existence of 'familiars'. A familiar was said to be a spirit or minor demon that appeared in animal form and acted as a servant, spy and companion to the witch it accompanied. It was also credited with magical abilities, such as bewitching enemies or changing shape.

The animals most commonly associated with this belief were black cats and black dogs, but a familiar could also be a snake, mouse, ferret, hare, bat or bird, particularly a raven or an owl. A witch was said to acquire a familiar as part of her initiation into witchcraft.

The witch hunts of the 16th and 17th centuries are the likeliest source of the belief that black cats are bad luck, and could be why some people fear black dogs. Unfortunately, even though the witch hunts are long over, the superstitions they created still remain, and many black cats and dogs in animal shelters have trouble finding homes.

MODERN MYSTERIES

Today, we like to think that we've outgrown the myths and superstitions about animals that have no basis in fact. But have we really explained everything animals can do? Some mysteries are still unsolved when it comes to animals and the incredible abilities they really do seem to have.

Part of the reason for this is the way we've viewed animals historically. Until recently, we assumed that humans were the only species to live in complex social systems, to experience emotions like empathy or have a sense of right and wrong, to use language to communicate, and to possess problem-solving skills. With more research now being undertaken to understand animals, we have had to give them much more credit than before. For example, a recent study reported in *Animal Cognition* showed that chickens have at least 24 different vocalizations and demonstrate both self-control and guile. Animals are clearly smarter and more complex than we ever imagined.

Dolphins are often perceived as one of the most socially complex and intelligent mammals after human beings.

Understanding how animals do what they do also forces us to accept our own limitations as humans. There are animals that can see, smell and hear things beyond the reach of our senses. What seems like a psychic ability to detect something invisible or find something that's missing might simply be a case of the animal using its senses, which are far superior to ours.

That doesn't mean we have everything animals do figured out, however. Animals present us with new mysteries to solve every day, and they may have abilities that we are yet to uncover. Sometimes it seems as if they can communicate without making a sound or somehow sense what their human companions are doing miles away. It will take much more research and observation to put the clues together and understand what is really going on when animals perform amazing feats.

When it comes to our pet animals, particularly dogs and cats, the matter can be even more complicated because of the strong emotional ties we have with them. Do they really understand us as well as we believe they do, or are we simply humanizing them and attributing thoughts to them that aren't there? Is there a psychic bond between pets and their people that helps them to find us when they're lost, or know instinctively when something is wrong with us, or are we giving out clues that they can read without us realizing it?

In this book we will look at some of the abilities, skills and mysteries of the animal kingdom. We will explain what can be explained, and muse on the mysteries still to be solved. We'll look at how animals use their talents to help us in so many different ways: offering us comfort, assisting those of us who need it, finding us when we get lost and sometimes laying down their lives to protect ours. If you were an animal lover before you picked up this book (and who isn't), you will be even more amazed by our furry friends by the time you reach the end.

A LUCKY BLACK CAT

April Hubbard and her cat Seymour had a bond that went beyond the normal affection between cat and owner. April adopted Seymour after her sister,

Seymour the black cat with the power of awareness for his owner's pain and the ability to demonstrate sympathy pains with his owner, April.

who worked at a local veterinary clinic, brought him over for a visit. Seymour, a mature black, long-haired cat, had been rescued from a junkyard where he'd been badly abused. He'd been beaten, slashed with a box-cutter and nearly set on fire. After several months of recovery at the clinic, he was finally well enough to find a new home and April offered hers.

April was no stranger to pain herself. She'd developed spinal cord tumours at the age of sixteen and, despite multiple surgeries, her condition was chronic and degenerative. As April came to depend on Seymour for comfort, he also came to depend on her. After a year together, April's health took a sharp turn for the worse and she was rushed to hospital in the middle of the night. Her sister moved in with Seymour, who wandered around crying and searching for April. After a couple of weeks his black fur started to turn grey around the neck. A month after April left for the hospital, Seymour had turned from the darkest black to completely grey. A vet found him to be in perfect health, and the only explanation for the change was that he was stressed from the separation. April spent three months in the hospital. Within three weeks of her return home, Seymour's fur returned to its natural black colour.

Once April was back home, Seymour became hyper-aware of where she felt pain. Each morning she would wake up to Seymour gently crossing his paws over the place where the pain was greatest. Some days it would be her leg, other days it was her back or sometimes her head, but each day before she was even aware of the pain, Seymour understood where it hurt and he would press his warm body right there to try to comfort her.

The relationship between April and Seymour had an unusual intensity, perhaps because of Seymour's suffering in his earlier years. For April, having a black cat enter her life was the best luck she could imagine.

DID YOU KNOW?

The question of whether animals possess psychic abilities or extrasensory perception (ESP) has actually been investigated by scientists. From the 1950s through to the 1970s a variety of experiments were undertaken using cats, mice, gerbils and dogs, to name a few. At the time, there was a lot of popular interest in parapsychology, ESP, psychics and other unexplained phenomena. However, nearly all of the studies were published in *The Journal of Parapsychology*, and the fact that only this particular journal accepted the studies makes it difficult to trust the results. This is especially true because all of the published studies seemed to conclude that they had found evidence of ESP in the animals.

ANIMAL GPS

If someone dropped you off in a strange town hundreds of miles from home, could you find your way back without a map or GPS? Most people would find it a challenge, if not impossible. But for many animals, a sense of direction and a homing instinct are completely natural. Consider monarch butterflies: they make their way from Canada to Mexico, arriving at a specific wintering location, even though they've never been there before. Sea turtles return to the very same beach where they were born when it's time to lay their eggs, leaving the ocean for the first time since they crawled in on their first day of life. Dogs that have been lost in the woods during a family vacation sometimes turn up at home months later, hundreds of miles from where they started.

All of this sounds rather magical and mysterious. These animals have never seen a map, they haven't been taught the route by their parents or other members of their species, and yet they know where to go. How is this possible? Is it all down to instinct or is there something else that helps them find their way over incredibly long distances?

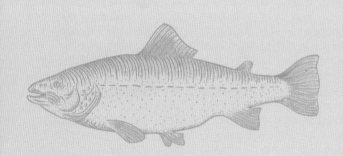

The answers are complicated, and in some cases we don't fully understand them yet. What we do know is that different animals use different navigational methods and abilities to get where they need to go.

GATHERING INFORMATION

Animals gather information about where they are, and where they're going, in a huge number of ways. Most animals cleverly use more than one of these information-gathering methods to find their way, because the more information you can gather, the more accurate your navigation will be.

Magnetic fields Lots of animals, including some migrating birds and insects, bats and possibly even cats, can use Earth's magnetic fields to help them navigate. They can feel the changes in the magnetic fields, and use this information to determine whether they are headed the right way to get home.

Visual clues Obviously animals can use recognition of landmarks and other familiar objects to help guide them. In a study by Oxford University, tracking devices attached to homing pigeons showed that for journeys that had been repeated several times, the birds preferred to follow main roads rather than travelling 'as the crow flies', presumably to simplify decision-making. The position of the sun in the sky, combined with knowing what time of day it is based on circadian rhythms (natural waking/sleeping cycles), can also provide valuable clues to animals about their position. This method has been linked to navigation by fish, sea turtles, butterflies and other insects. Other animals can see things that we can't. Bees, for example, can see polarized light, which helps to guide them in ways that would be completely invisible to us.

Night-time navigation Even at night, a lot of animals gather visual clues to tell them where they are. Just like sailors, some animals can navigate using the stars as their map. These animals include migrating birds, seals and even the lowly dung beetle. The position of a particularly bright star, or a pattern of stars (such as a constellation) can help the animals to keep on a straight path when there's no sun to guide them and it's too dark to see landmarks. You might find this hard to believe, but the theory that birds navigate using the stars has been tested by researchers using a planetarium to simulate the night sky. By using a simulated version of the stars in the sky, they could tell that the birds were definitely using star positions to help them, and not just other clues that were available outside such as landmarks or smells.

Currents and pressures For birds and flying insects, the air pressure and air currents also provide valuable information. This is especially true during long-distance migrations, where following a known air current could not only direct the birds to the right spot, but also give them a helping hand by pushing them along with a tail wind. For animals such as whales, fish and turtles that navigate through water, ocean currents and water temperature changes can provide the same type of information about their location and direction.

Salmon swim against the current to return to their birthplace. They use their sense of smell to determine the location where they were spawned.

Scent When it comes to dogs (and some other animals) the key to navigation is all in the nose. By finding and following familiar scents, dogs can navigate back home from surprisingly far away. Even when home itself is too far away to smell, dogs can find areas where familiar people or animals have recently been, allowing them to follow a trail of overlapping scents until they return to familiar territory. And dogs aren't the only animals sniffing out the right path. 'Olfactory navigation' – navigating by smell – is thought to be part of the pigeon's toolbox when it comes to locating home from far away. Even salmon, which return to their place of birth to spawn, are believed to use smell to guide them back to the right river, since every river has a distinct aroma.

Spatial orientation Vestibular senses are the complex systems that make us aware of acceleration and tilt, and help us to keep our balance. For humans, these systems reside in the inner ear. Vestibular navigation is an important tool for a lot of animals. It enables birds, for example, to be able to judge whether they are flying at a constant height, and whether they are being blown off course by the wind. It also helps animals to recognize how fast they are travelling, which will let them know how far they've gone.

GOING THE DISTANCE

With this collection of tools at their disposal, animals perform some amazing feats of navigation. Let's look at some examples.

Birds are among the best navigators on the planet, often migrating thousands of miles every year between summer and winter habitats. Some have exceptional homing abilities, and can find their way back home over seemingly impossible distances. For example, researchers working with a large seabird called the Laysan albatross discovered that it could find its home on Midway Island in the Pacific Ocean from 5,100 kilometres (3,200 miles) away, a journey that lasted 10 days. Homing pigeons, which are trained to return to their home base from wherever they are released, can travel up to 700 miles (1,126 kilometres) in a single day and stay in the air for up to 16 hours. This remarkable endurance, combined with their equally remarkable homing abilities, means that they can get home over very long distances. In the late 19th century, a story emerged about a pigeon that was released in northern Africa and made its way home to England, over 7,000 miles (11,000 kilometres) away. But it's the Arctic tern that holds the record for the longest annual migration. These birds literally fly across the world, covering a round-trip distance of 50,000 miles (80,000 kilometres) every year between their breeding grounds in the Arctic and the Southern Ocean (and thereby experiencing an enviable two summers a year and no winters).

Whales often have predictable migration routes and travel long distances between their feeding areas and their mating grounds. Humpback whales might even be the most seasoned travellers of the sea. Their migration routes can cover distances of 6,000 miles (9,600 kilometres) between their tropical mating areas near the Equator and their more frigid feeding locations to the north and south. Reaching the right breeding area is essential for the survival of many whale species. If they couldn't find the right meeting spots, the whales would be widely scattered around the oceans and be unable to find mates.

The instinctive drive for sea turtles to return to the beach where they were born to lay eggs can make for some astounding journeys too. Researchers tracked one leatherback turtle from Indonesia all the way to Oregon, a journey of over 12,400 miles (20,000 kilometres).

Monarch butterflies are also famous for their long migrations, travelling nearly 4,000 kilometres (2,500 miles) each way between their summer feeding and mating areas in the United States and Canada and their tropical winter retreat in Mexico, taking several generations to complete the return journey. Less well known are the long flights undertaken by the dragonfly. Many species of this majestic insect migrate across the Indian Ocean from India to Africa.

Long migration patterns are impressive when the animals involved fly or swim, but it can be even tougher to cover vast distances on paw or hoof. The longest migration pattern of any land mammal belongs to the barren-ground caribou and some populations of woodland caribou. Living in Canada's far north, these animals travel up to 3,100 miles (5,000 kilometres) every year in search of grass and moss to graze on. During these migrations they are exposed to predators such as wolves, coyotes, lynx and bears.

HOMEWARD BOUND

We've all heard the classic tales about dogs and cats that have been lost, left behind or given to a new home, only to find their way home against all odds. Some of these stories have even been made into movies. While it's true that a lot of dogs and cats have amazing navigational skills, it doesn't guarantee that every lost pet will find its way home. As many heartbroken pet owners can attest, often a lost pet is lost forever. Just as some people have a great sense of direction and others can't find their way out of a cardboard box, some pets are better at finding their homes than others.

Cats are known for their ability to find their way home. In fact, it can become a big problem when their families move to a new house. This is because cats generally don't like change, and a new house is a big change. Cat owners sometimes discover after moving that their cat has been returning to their old house. This happens so often that vets and other experts advise owners to keep their cats indoors for the first couple of weeks after a move, until the cat has accepted the new house. Unlike dogs, cats can be more attached to their places than their people. Dogs would lose interest in the old house after realizing that their people are somewhere else but cats can take a while to accept that their home is somewhere new. This isn't true of all cats, though. There are tales of cats travelling miles to find their owners who have moved into places where cats aren't allowed, been admitted to hospitals or simply left them with a new owner.

Some research has been done to test the homing abilities of cats. Back in 1922, a mother cat was used for testing because she would have a strong motivation to get home to her kittens. (Animal research ethics were not as strict back then.) The cat was placed in a sack, then transported in a car to a location 1.6–11.3 kilometres (1–7 miles) from home. The drop-off locations were different each time, but the cat was always able to find its way home. After seven successful trials, the researchers increased the distance to 16½ miles (26.5 kilometres) but the cat was not able to find her way home from that distance.

A cat's ability to find home may be influenced by how long he or she has been away. In a 1954 experiment, cats were tested using a maze in a laboratory to see whether they would quickly orient themselves in the direction of their homes. The cats that were returned home between tests did a better job of pointing themselves towards home than the cats that were kept at the laboratory for longer periods.

Cats have an innate capacity to orientate themselves and to navigate over enormous distances to find their way home.

It will be no surprise to hear that when dogs need to find their way home, they often follow their noses. We sometimes don't realize just how far away scent can be detected, because humans are particularly bad at it. But for a dog, a smell over 3 kilometres (2 miles) away is not impossible to locate and follow.

Stories abound of dogs finding their way home over hundreds of miles. Obviously they can't smell home from that far away, so how do they do it? Researchers think that dogs use all the clues at their disposal to put the puzzle together. Overlapping areas of scents, which provide clues to where their people have been, are probably the main way they find the right direction. If their owners stop for meals, petrol or overnight stays, there will be scent clues left behind. They may also recognize the smell of familiar animals along the way, letting them know they're on the right track.

Landmarks and memorizing a path may also help in some cases. If a dog remembers passing a particular place on the way they may recall that place when they pass it on the way back home. If they remember heading in particular directions and making certain turns on the way, they can use that information to find their way back. Studies with dogs have found that they will try to find what they are looking for first by taking a direct path to where they think it should be (dead reckoning) and if that isn't possible they will try to use landmarks and other clues to backtrack along the path they travelled. Both of these methods of navigation are helpful if the dog is finding the way home from somewhere they have been before, or somewhere they arrived at on foot, so that the dog was able to absorb information about the route or observed landmarks along the way. These skills (which one study shows can be improved with practice) combined with a dog's remarkable sense of smell can account for many occasions when lost dogs manage to find their homes and are happily reunited with their families.

MISSING HER MUM

Elda lived in the small town of Armstrong, British Columbia, Canada, with her beautiful Sheltie cross, Samantha. The two were very close, but Elda knew that it was time for her to give up her house and move into the local aged care home – a home where pets were not permitted.

Samantha was adopted by a couple who lived in the same town, and she went to live in their house with a fenced yard. Although Elda was sad to lose her friend, she felt this was the best thing she could do for Samantha. Elda moved into the new home and tried to adapt to her new life.

A year later, Elda was surprised to see a dog run into her room and jump up onto her bed. To her amazement, it was Samantha. She waited for the dog's

The Shetland sheepdog is known for its fine pedigree, beautiful coat and, as in the case of Samantha the Sheltie cross, its incredible instinct for locating its owner.

new owners to come in, but it soon became clear that Samantha had come on her own. She had escaped from their house by digging her way out of the fenced yard and found her way to her former owner in a building she'd only visited once, nearly a year earlier. Not only did she find the building (and sneak in repeatedly after staff members kicked her out) but she made her way to Elda's new room, which was not the room she was in when Samantha first visited.

Their happy reunion was bittersweet, since Elda knew that she would have to send Samantha back. But the home's staff and residents fell in love with the sweet dog and let her stay on for a few days. The residents enjoyed walking her, playing with her and reminiscing about their own former pets.

During this time, Samantha actually prevented a late-night burglary by barking to alert staff to an intruder, and scaring the man off. That pretty much sealed the deal for the loyal dog. The staff and residents took a vote and altered their rules to allow Samantha to stay with her beloved owner.

Samantha somehow had remembered the route to her owner's new home for nearly a year after just one visit, showing impressive spatial awareness and memory skills. The little dog also showed remarkable devotion and determination to be reunited with her favourite person.

DID YOU KNOW?

Once in a while, animals find their way to places where they have never been before in order to find their owners who have moved or travelled without them. People continue to search for ways to explain how they do it. Most animals left behind by their owners, or lost just before a long move, never make it back to their families unless a good Samaritan steps in to help reunite them. But once in a while, a remarkable story of devotion and determination arises, raising the question of how the animal knew where to look.

This mysterious phenomenon was dubbed 'psi-trailing' by a parapsychologist named Dr Joseph Banks Rhine. He believed that some animals shared a strong psychic or telepathic link with their owners, which allowed them to find their beloved people in unknown locations. Psi-trailing abilities have been attributed to both cats and dogs in various parts of the world. There is no known explanation for some instances of psi-trailing, where the distance involved and the modes of transportation would make it impossible for the animals to track their owners by scent or by familiar landmarks.

Theories include a sort of magnetic attraction between a pet and its owner, which is disturbed when they are separated. As the animal moves closer to the location of the owner, this disturbance subsides, letting the animal know he or she is on the right path. Of course, there's no more evidence for this theory than there is for the belief that the owner and pet have a telepathic or psychic connection. Pets miraculously finding their owners in new, far-away places remains one of the great mysteries of animal navigation.

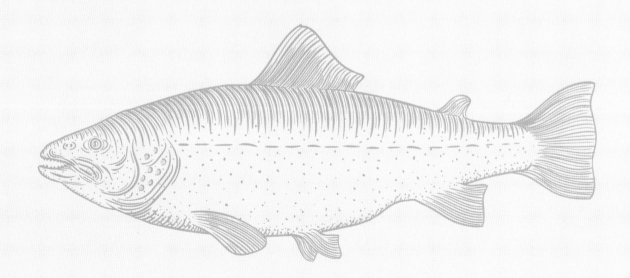

ANIMALS TO THE RESCUE

Searching for someone lost in the wilderness, buried under an avalanche or trapped under the rubble of a collapsed building can seem like an impossible task. Search teams try to explore the most likely places, but with every hour that passes the chances of a successful rescue become smaller and smaller.

Thankfully, there are animals that have been specially trained to help us undertake these daunting missions. They can use their superior sense of smell combined with speed and agility to cover much more ground far more effectively than human search volunteers. They have saved countless lives all over the world in the wake of disasters large and small.

FROM ST BERNARDS TO BATTLEFIELDS

The classic image of the rescue dog is that of a sturdy St Bernard in the snow, searching for lost and freezing travellers. These gentle giants were indeed the first dogs to be intentionally used for search-and-rescue work.

Their story begins in the Alps. The Great St Bernard Pass was a dangerous mountain route between Italy and Switzerland. A group of monks had built a hospice to accommodate travellers using the pass, and they were aware that people often got into trouble and lost their way in the snow. While their first dogs (acquired between 1660 and 1670) were meant to be watchdogs and companions, they also helped the monks look for lost or injured travellers. The large dogs were descended from mastiff breeds that had come to the area during Roman times.

These dogs proved so good at finding travellers that they were eventually sent out on their own when the conditions were poor, working in pairs or trios. If the dogs located a lost or injured traveller, one dog would stay with the person while the other one or two returned to the hospice to get help. The system was in place by the mid-1700s and the dogs performed rescues on the pass for 150 years. The dogs were later named for the pass they protected for so many years, and became known as St Bernards.

In many depictions, St Bernards are shown with a small cask attached to their collars. Legend says that this cask was filled with brandy to warm the people they found in the snowy pass. There's no evidence that this was actually the case, and in fact it would have led to a higher chance of hypothermia because alcohol brings the blood closer to the surface of the body where it would cool down faster. But old legends are hard to ignore, and even today the image of the heroic St Bernard with his wooden cask endures.

In the late 19th century, the military became interested in using dogs for search-and-rescue purposes. They began training dogs to search battlefields for survivors and alert medics to their location. During the First World War this was put into action across the European front. Dogs would either be trained to

A St Bernard dog with a traditional cask attached to his collar sits ready for a rescue operation.

sit with the injured soldier and bark for help, or to return to the medic and lead him to the soldier. This saved a lot of lives because the dogs were able to find injured soldiers in the dark or in places where they were difficult to see.

In Britain during the Second World War, search and rescue moved from the battlefield to the city. Dogs sometimes helped after an area had been bombed, searching for survivors in the rubble of damaged or collapsed buildings. The dogs could pinpoint where the survivors were trapped, allowing rescue workers to reach them more quickly. This type of work would eventually become known as 'urban search and rescue'. Famous dogs who worked in London during the Blitz include Rip, a terrier cross, who worked in the East End, and Jet, a German Shepherd (Alsatian). Both dogs each located at least 100 people buried in rubble and were later awarded the Dickin medal for their bravery (see also page 35).

The modern search-and-rescue system, using mainly volunteer handlers and their dogs in a variety of situations, wasn't fully established until the 1970s. Now there are associations around the world that provide training to recognized standards and organize deployments of teams wherever they are needed.

Rip, the famous terrier cross who helped locate and rescue many people during the Blitz, sits on top of debris at a bombsite in London.

HOW DOGS SNIFF US OUT

Finding someone lost in a vast wilderness or buried under snow seems like an impossible task. How do search-and-rescue dogs manage to do it? Human searchers have limited abilities when it comes to this type of rescue. We can only look for visual signs that the person is nearby (smoke from a fire, footprints, etc.) or shout loudly and hope to hear a response. Dogs, however, use their amazing noses to search far more efficiently than people can.

There are essentially two ways that dogs can be trained to search for people: tracking and trailing. Tracking involves the dog sniffing ground to detect distrubances in the surfaces to assess where the subjects foot steps (or tracks) may lead. Usually, this is not very effective on hard surfaces like concrete where there is no disturbed earth for the dog to smell.

Dogs are trained to do this by first tracking someone they know. The dog is rewarded with praise, play and treats for finding the person. Gradually, treats are eliminated so that the dog searches for a play reward only. The searches are made gradually longer and more difficult, and eventually the dog learns to search for strangers.

To be successful at this, a dog needs to have strong work and prey drives, but also be trained to ignore distractions such as the scent of other animals. A lot of training is required to teach a dog reliable tracking and trailing skills and, since search-and-rescue teams are normally volunteers, it takes a huge commitment from handlers to keep their dogs ready to be called into action.

Trailing is slightly different. People shed around 40,000 skin cells every minute, and each of those cells carries our individual scent. Dogs can be trained to follow the scent trail we leave behind, even when there's no obvious path along the ground. Trailing is important in situations such as avalanches, where the path that the missing person has travelled on is buried, and in urban search and rescue, where things have moved around during an earthquake or other disaster.

As difficult as it is to believe, air scenting can even be used to search for people underwater. Water search dogs are taken out in boats to try to locate the scent of bodily gases that rise up from the water. They are used with teams of divers who can search below the location indicated by the dog, saving search time. Since the missing people are underwater, this type of search technique is only used for recovering victims, not for finding people who are still alive.

The best search-and-rescue dogs are from working breeds because they have the drive and stamina required for long, tedious searches. Dogs can be worked for hours at a time trying to locate a missing person before night falls or the temperature drops too low. Some of the most common breeds used are border collies, German shepherds, labradors and golden retrievers.

An old purebred German Shepherd searches the grass.

SEARCHING IN THE SNOW

When a person is buried during an avalanche, every minute counts. Survival becomes almost impossible after just 30 minutes under the snow, but finding someone who has been buried is incredibly difficult. It normally involves searchers with long poles wandering around the avalanche area and poking their poles randomly into the snow to see whether they hit anything. It's a slow and painstaking process.

Specially trained search-and-rescue dogs can increase the odds of finding someone alive after an avalanche. The dog's hunting drive is used as the basis for the search. Dogs are initially trained to look for people hiding in hollowed-out piles of snow and rewarded with play for their successes. They need to dig into the snow to rescue the 'victims', which teaches them to indicate by digging when they find someone during a search. Once they are good at finding people in the big snow piles, they learn to find people who are buried below the surface, where there is no visual cue to look for.

RESCUE FROM THE RUBBLE

Not all search-and-rescue missions take place in the wilderness. After a natural or man-made disaster in a town or city, finding survivors is a race against time. Urban search and rescue, known as USAR, combines people, dogs and often heavy equipment to save as many lives as possible. The situations where USAR teams are called in include earthquakes, tornadoes, hurricanes, bombings, fires and mudslides. Any time buildings have collapsed or people have been trapped in an urban setting, USAR is deployed. You could say that these teams are direct descendants of those who worked in London during the Blitz, and dogs like Rip and Jet.

In these situations, it is difficult for human rescuers to do an effective job on their own. Rubble is often unstable, and moving it to look for survivors can cause things to shift and endanger both survivors and rescuers. Dogs can scramble over and through the rubble with much less disturbance. They use air-scenting skills and their excellent hearing to determine where people are trapped and guide rescuers to the right area so that they can begin to remove debris.

Dogs also help to keep rescuers safe by letting them know which buildings not to search. If the dog cannot find any human scent to follow, rescuers can skip that building and reduce their chances of being injured. In large-scale disasters such as earthquakes or hurricanes, narrowing down the number of buildings to search for survivors allows limited resources to be put to the best use, which saves more lives.

EARTHQUAKE ESCAPES

In 2011, the city of Christchurch, New Zealand experienced a strong earthquake that damaged many buildings and caused two high-rises to collapse. The city's famed cathedral also partly toppled, and there were fears that people might have been trapped in the popular tourist attraction. The search-and-rescue effort began immediately and included all available certified dog and handler teams with USAR training.

The first teams that were on the scene put in nearly 30 hours of work before other teams began to arrive from around the country. The New Zealand USAR teams of 7 handlers and 10 dogs investigated over 80 sites in and around Christchurch during the first crucial days when survivors were most likely to

Christchurch USAR rescue dog Boss helped to search damaged properties during the aftermath of the February 2011 earthquake.

be found. The search dogs had to be agile over rubble, to climb ladders and planks to access search areas, to search independently in structurally unsound buildings by following their handlers' voice directions, and most importantly to bark strongly at the scent of trapped people. All the while, they were working in terrible conditions and in danger from a series of aftershocks.

USAR dog teams later arrived from Australia, Japan and Singapore to assist with the searches. In total, the USAR operation lasted for 28 days and involved over 500 people, making it the largest in the country's history. There were several successful rescues in very challenging circumstances. While the rescue effort was underway, the region continued to be shaken by serious aftershocks, putting the dogs and handlers in constant danger.

DID YOU KNOW?

While most search-and-rescue work involves teams of dogs and handlers, there are also search-and-rescue horses. Horses have a lot going for them when it comes to search and rescue. First, they can help people cover a lot of ground in areas where vehicles can't go – horses are sure on their feet and good at picking out a path so that their riders can focus on searching and not worry too much about watching where they're going. Secondly, horses actually have quite a good sense of smell (almost as good as a dog's) and excellent hearing, which they normally use to alert them to possible predators. Their sensitivity to strange smells and sounds means that their behaviour will change when there is something unexpected in the area. This can indicate when there's a lost person nearby.

Horses can be trained for scent detection, although this is still relatively uncommon. Historically, scenting was used by horses and riders to locate prey on hunting trips, to find water and to warn people of approaching danger. Horses are unlikely to replace dogs as search-and-rescue experts, but in the future they may be recognized as another tool at the searchers' disposal.

COURAGE AND CAMARADERIE

When you think of military animals, horses immediately come to mind. Before the 20th century, an army with a strong cavalry had a huge advantage over its adversaries. Horses allowed an army to move faster, carry more supplies and overpower the enemy. But modern technology has made the cavalry largely obsolete. Between the two World Wars their role in the world's great battles gradually became a piece of history. Tanks and trucks are now more effective modes of transportation, and horses can no longer keep up. These days, horses play a mainly ceremonial role in the military. They participate in parades and other events, but are no longer used in combat.

Horses were not alone in helping an army gain advantage. Messenger pigeons were an important military tool in the First and Second World Wars. Trained homing pigeons delivered messages silently over distances of up to 700 miles (1,126 kilometres) in a day, and were harder to intercept than radio transmissions. They were also harder for the enemy to target and kill than human messengers. In fact, this work was considered so vital to the war effort that the heraldry of the pigeons was not overlooked and 32 received the Dickin medal for valour for their work during the Second World War. One of these pigeons, called Winkie, saved the lives of an aircraft crew who were forced to ditch into the North Sea on the way back from a mission but managed to release Winkie as they were going down.

In 1944, Maria Dickin, founder of the People's Dispensary for Sick Animals (PDSA) veterinary charity, presented RAF homing pigeon Winkie with the Dickin medal, which recognizes the contribution of animals in wartime.

The UK and US armies have stopped using pigeons, but other countries have not given up on the idea. The Chinese military continues to train thousands of homing pigeons to this day, in case modern communication methods are destroyed or infiltrated during a war. The Austrian military reportedly used pigeons to communicate during the war in Iraq in the early 2000s. Aware that their radio transmissions were being overheard by the enemy, they took a step back in time and put their faith in these winged messengers. The French army also maintains a small flock of 150 trained homing pigeons, and they believe that around 20,000 more are kept by French hobbyists and could be called upon in times of war to serve their country. Could the homing pigeon become a common military animal again worldwide? Modern warfare tactics might make it a good idea to be prepared in the event of a blackout of electronic and satellite communications.

An American scientist developed a unique job for pigeons during the Second World War. One of the difficulties the Allied forces faced was improving the targeting systems for their missiles. Animal behaviourist and inventor B. F. Skinner came up with a plan he called Project Pigeon. His idea was to put pigeons into the nosecones of missiles after training them, by means of a food reward system, to peck at the image of their intended target, such as a German battleship, which the pigeons would see as they approached. The touch-sensitive screens controlled the steering system of the missile and kept it on course. As crazy as it sounds, the system seemed to work. But other technologies were developed at the same time and the pigeon missiles were never tested in battle conditions. It's probably just as well, since it would have been a suicide mission for the pigeons.

While pigeons are making a tentative comeback as messengers (but not as guidance systems), the use of military and police dogs is more widespread than ever around the world. But if you think dogs are a recent addition to the armed forces, you're mistaken. There are stories of dogs in battle dating back to the Roman Empire. Wearing chain mail and spiked collars, these dogs were used to attack the enemy's horses, forcing their riders to the ground.

Later, around the beginning of the 19th century, armies started using dogs' superior sense of smell as an early warning system. Dogs were stationed outside important encampments or fortresses, waiting for the enemy to arrive. As soon as they could smell unfamiliar soldiers in the area, the dogs would bark to warn people of the approaching danger. The dogs made it very difficult to launch a surprise attack, and gave the defending soldiers crucial time to get ready for battle.

Over the years, dogs have taken on more and more duties in military units, and now in police units as well. They are often hailed as heroes, and receive medals for bravery.

TODAY'S MILITARY DOGS

Dogs have a lot of different jobs in today's military. Their extreme loyalty, excellent sense of smell, physical strength and ability to get into small places makes them versatile soldiers, able to do things that their human counterparts can't. Dogs are no longer expected to dress in spiked armour, but sometimes they do wear bulletproof vests.

Most military dogs belong to just a few breeds: German shepherds, Dutch shepherds and Belgian Malinois (a breed similar to German shepherds). These breeds are intelligent, hard-working, physically strong and not easily distracted. Other breeds, such as hunting dogs, may have better noses, but they can get led astray by their instincts and end up chasing prey animals instead of enemy soldiers!

Whatever job they will eventually be assigned, military dogs go through several months of intensive training. Any dogs found to be too aggressive, hard to train, physically inferior, easily distracted or unable to perform their duties consistently are weeded out during the training period. Most dogs are trained by one specific handler, who stays with the dog throughout its service career. The bond between dog and handler is very strong, ensuring that duties are carried out without question.

Military dogs can be trained to sniff out specific things, such as explosives. By finding hidden bombs and other devices, dogs can save hundreds of lives. Explosives dogs can be deployed in war zones, and in other high-risk areas such as airports or even tourist attractions that may be targeted by terrorists. The dogs can pinpoint the smell of chemicals used in explosives even if they have been hidden or buried in other strong-smelling materials. They can find explosives under the ground, in luggage, on people and in buildings.

Other dogs are trained to sniff out human scents. These dogs are used to identify nearby enemy soldiers in order to warn their unit when there are enemies waiting to ambush them. Sentry dogs are sent out ahead of infantry units, staying silent and hidden as they patrol for enemy soldiers. When the sentry dogs find a scent, they stand stiff to indicate that the enemy is near, without making any noise to give their presence away. They can detect people up to 915 metres (1000 yards) away when the wind is blowing in the right direction. Not only do dogs have a far better sense of smell than people, they also have better hearing. If they don't smell enemy activity, they may still be able to detect the sound of distant troops or of enemy scouts moving through the area.

Some dogs still hold their centuries-old role as early warning systems. They are stationed at military posts and other important locations such as arsenals and airfields, and they sound the alarm when there are people approaching. During the Second World War, the US military used over 9,000 dogs in these sentry roles, many of them protecting harbours and coastal areas.

Another traditional job for a dog's nose is finding injured soldiers. After a battle, dogs locate casualties in locations where they are hard to find, getting medical help to them in time to save their lives. When every minute counts, casualty dogs can make a huge difference.

While it's easy to think of a military dog as a sort of 'walking nose', they do other important jobs that don't involve their sense of smell. For example, dogs are often used to intimidate or subdue enemy soldiers without the use of force. Simply the presence of a large, growling dog can make people think twice about trying to attack or escape.

Another specialized duty for dogs is acting as messengers between two groups of soldiers. These dogs are trained to move quietly and use natural cover to hide themselves as they deliver messages between two designated people. In a situation where radio communication is not safe, a messenger dog may be the best way to communicate over a moderate distance.

POLICE DOGS

It has been just over 100 years since the police started to employ dogs in an organized and consistent way. In the late 1800s, police in London began to use bloodhounds to help them track suspects. It is said that this began with the search for the infamous serial killer Jack the Ripper. By the early 20th century, Belgium and Germany were training dogs to work with their police forces. Since then, almost every country in the world has made dogs a part of their police force.

Dogs working with police perform similar roles to those working with the military, but often in very different circumstances. Some police forces train each police dog to perform one specific task, such as finding explosives. Others train the dogs in multiple tasks, depending on how many dogs they are able to train and how isolated an area they work in. While a major city might have lots of police dogs with specific roles, a rural area might have only one or two dogs that they can use and it helps if those dogs are trained to do a few different tasks.

Tracking a suspect or an escaped prisoner has long been on the job list for police dogs. Dogs can track a human scent if they are led to a known starting point, such as the scene of a crime from which a suspect has fled. In other cases, a dog can be given a scent to track, perhaps from an item of clothing belonging to the person they need to find (see How dogs sniff us out, page 33). This works well when there is no clear trail, such as looking for a kidnapping victim.

Researchers trying to pin down how dogs can determine one person's scent from another's have found support for the theory that every person has a genetic scent signature that is as unique as their fingerprints. If a scenting dog, especially a bloodhound, is presented with an item that carries a person's scent, they can identify that unique scent among many others. Dogs can do this with extreme accuracy if the scent item was worn or touched by the person within 24 hours of the search. As the scent on the item fades over a number of days or weeks, it becomes more difficult for the dog to pinpoint the person it belongs to. A dog's nose is considered so reliable when it comes to recognizing an individual's scent that their identification of a suspect is admissible in court in many places.

If you believe what you see in the movies, one of the best ways to throw a police dog off your trail is to walk through a stream or cross a river because there is no ground for your scent to lie on. But the movies aren't always accurate – in reality, your scent lingers not just on the ground but also in the air where you have been. If the dog is not too far behind you, he or she can

A German shepherd military police dog walks beside his handler.

pick up your 'scent cone' in the air and follow it along the water's edge until a ground trail appears again.

Tracking and trailing dogs are also sometimes given the grisly task of finding human remains. These can be victims of foul play, people who got lost or hurt and subsequently died or people who died in an accident, attack or natural disaster. This important job helps police to catch killers, identify victims and give closure to families.

While some police dogs are trained to track and search for people, others are trained to pick up different scents. Explosives, firearms and narcotics are the main targets for police dogs. They aren't the only targets, though – in some countries, border control areas such as airports have biosecurity dogs that sniff out food and plants that might carry unwanted elements (such as foreign insects or plant diseases) into the country. Other dogs are trained to smell cash, catching people trying to hide large sums of money.

Narcotics dogs are trained to identify a wide range of drugs by their unique chemical scents, including marijuana, cocaine, heroin, methamphetamine and other substances. The dogs can find these scents even when they have been disguised by hiding the drugs in other strong-smelling substances such as coffee grounds or sealing them in air-tight containers. Narcotics dogs are often trained to find firearms too, because people running drug operations are also well armed in many cases.

Just like military dogs, the most common breeds for police dogs are German shepherds, Dutch shepherds and Belgian Malinois. They are well suited to this work because of their intelligence and high work drive. Once they are on the job they don't easily give up. Other breeds such as hounds and spaniels are sometimes used for scent work. This can be especially helpful in places where police do not want to make people feel nervous, such as an airport or a school. A more friendly-looking dog puts people at ease and makes the search easier.

Police dogs start training when they are about a year old. Until that time, they receive basic obedience and socialization training. If they have a high work drive and good temperament, they are sent for a medical exam before being selected for police training. Dogs are trained using play as a reward. When they complete their tasks, they get to play with a favourite toy. It's all the thanks they want for their hard work.

Canine trainers and handlers work very closely with just one or two dogs. In fact, police dogs often live with their handlers to strengthen their bond. They get to know each other so well that after a while the dog learns to pick up on things such as what equipment their handler is carrying to understand what task is coming. The dogs work when their handlers work, and are on vacation when their handlers are on vacation. It's a true partnership that lasts throughout the dog's working life, and often handlers keep their retired dogs as pets for the rest of the dogs' lives.

Drug detection dog Skye, from the Toronto Police Canine Unit, has an incredible nose for narcotics.

YOU CAN'T KEEP SECRETS FROM THE NOSE

Sergeant Sean Thrush was a member of the Toronto Police Canine Unit in Canada from 2008 to 2014. One day, Sean and his narcotics detection dog, Skye, were called to help the drug squad search a house. The police suspected that there would be a large quantity of drugs in the house, but after thoroughly searching every room they found only a small amount of marijuana. This wasn't the big stash they were looking for!

Skye and Sean began their search. On the main floor, they didn't find anything. But as they searched the finished basement of the house Skye began to dance around, indicating that she had found something.

She jumped up on a couch and started sniffing. But where Skye was indicating there was just a plain wall. No drawers to search, no bags or containers to look in, nothing to hide drugs underneath.

Had Skye made a mistake? Sean knew better than to doubt her. He told the drug squad that Skye had definitely picked up a scent in that spot. So the officers went to work searching the area until they found a hidden switch. The switch opened up a false wall to reveal a secret room, and the room was full of the narcotics Skye had indicated. The officers got their big bust, and they had Skye to thank. The hidden room had fooled their eyes, but not Skye's well-trained nose.

THE PDSA DICKIN MEDAL

The UK and US military have a specific medal that is awarded to animals for gallantry (outstanding courage) in combat. It was introduced in 1943 by Maria Dickin, founder of the People's Dispensary for Sick Animals (PDSA) to honour the work of animals in the Second World War and it is the animal equivalent of the Victoria Cross in the UK. The PDSA's website lists animals who have been awarded the honour, including Judy, a pointer who received the award in 1946 for 'magnificent courage and endurance in Japanese prison camps,' and Brian, a German shepherd (Alsatian) who received his award in 1947 after he parachuted into Normandy as part of the Allied invasion. He did so many jumps that he actually qualified as a paratrooper.

In 2016 the award was given to a dog called Lucca, who lost a leg while serving with the US Marines in Afghanistan. Lucca completed 400 missions during her six years with the US Marine Corps, and protected the lives of thousands of soldiers. On her final mission, an improvised explosive device (IED) exploded under her and badly damaged one of her front legs. It was the end of her military career, but she now lives as a pet with Gunnery Sgt Chris Willingham and his family. Willingham credits Lucca for keeping him safe in Afghanistan, and felt that giving her a wonderful life in retirement was the least he could do to thank her.

Corporal, and military dog-handler, Juan M. Rodriguez kneels next to Lucca, the eight-year-old Belgian Malinois who was deployed twice to Iraq and once to Afghanistan where she was injured by an improvised explosive device (IED). Her left front leg had to be amputated and she has since retired from military service. During her service, Lucca uncovered more than 40 improvised explosive devices and saved many lives.

AT YOUR SERVICE

If you've ever seen a blind person being led around town by their guide dog, you may have marvelled at how the dog seems to know exactly where to go and what to do. Guide dogs stop at red traffic lights, guide their owners around obstacles and ignore distractions that would have other dogs barking and chasing.

These dogs appear to be impossibly smart. They may even seem to be reading their owners' minds. But the truth is it all comes down to excellent training and a great attitude. Not every dog can be an assistance dog; it takes intelligence, focus, discipline and a good work ethic. People who use these dogs are extremely thankful for the hard work their dogs and the people who trained them have put in.

HOW DO THEY DO IT?

Assistance dogs, or service dogs, are often raised by a foster family for the first year of their lives. This family (or sometimes just one person) will socialize the dogs and teach them basic manners. Dogs need this time to grow and mature, and to calm down from their exuberant puppy behaviour, before taking on the intense training needed to become a service dog.

The training for different types of assistance dogs varies, but usually it involves a very intensive period of 4–6 months with specialized trainers. These trainers teach the dog tasks that will be important for their jobs as service dogs. For example, a guide dog for blind people will learn to cross the road safely, to redirect someone who is going the wrong way and to pick up items that have fallen and hand them back to the trainer. The training for a dog that will work with someone in a wheelchair might include opening doors by pulling on a rope, pushing buttons for automatic doors and elevators and putting items such as a wallet up on a shop counter. Trainers will eventually pretend to have the same limitations as the dogs future owners so that the dogs are prepared for their new jobs. All service dogs also learn that when they are wearing their vests or harnesses, it's work time. That means no barking at other dogs, chasing squirrels or playing fetch. They won't even respond when a stranger calls or pets them.

The final stage of training involves the dog's new owner. Often, the owner comes to the training facility for several weeks and works with the dog and the trainers until the owner and dog have a good understanding of each other's needs and personalities. Although the pieces have been put in place, the owners need to put in some hard work too. They need to be consistent and clear so that their dog understands what is wanted. A confused assistance dog might get frustrated and do the wrong thing.

Training an assistance dog is both time-consuming and expensive. Thankfully, a lot of generous people donate to organizations that train dogs so that the owners don't have to bear the full cost. In some cases, the owners will not need to pay for anything except the normal upkeep of their dog (food, vet bills and so forth).

The total cost of buying, raising and training a service dog is expensive. For example, it costs over £25,000 to train a British guide dog, and there are other ongoing expenses such as additional training. With so much cost and effort involved, it's not surprising that there are also long waiting lists for many types of assistance dogs.

A black Labrador assistance dog during the final stages of training.

Assistance dogs are also a big responsibility. For someone who is already dealing with a disability such as blindness or paralysis, taking care of a dog is no easy task. The dog needs to be fed and cared for, and of course the owner needs to clean up their dog's messes. Stoop and scoop is a lot more challenging when you can't see where the dog has pooped, or you need to pick it up while you're in a wheelchair. There's also the need to remind strangers not to pet or feed your dog while he or she is working. For this reason, it can be a big leap for someone with a disability to start using an assistance dog. The improvement in their quality of life has to outweigh the inconveniences of caring for a dog.

SPECIAL DOGS FOR SPECIAL NEEDS

You can usually recognize assistance dogs because they wear either a special vest that tells you they are working or a sturdy harness, and sometimes both. In most countries, these dogs are allowed to accompany their owners into places where dogs aren't normally allowed. They go into shops, restaurants, doctors' offices, schools, workplaces and pretty much anywhere else their owners need to be. There are a lot of situations in which assistance dogs are used.

Hearing loss Hearing dogs help people who are deaf or have profound hearing loss. The dogs are trained to alert their owners to important sounds such as a knock at the door, a fire alarm, the oven timer or a crying baby. The dogs can also learn to recognize their owner's names and alert them when someone is trying to get their attention. Unlike most other service dogs, hearing dogs tend to be small or medium breeds because they don't need to perform physical tasks. Often, they are adopted from animal shelters and trained to work with deaf owners.

Sight loss Guide dogs, sometimes known as seeing-eye dogs, need to be larger breeds so that they are tall enough to guide their owners around. The most common breeds for guide dogs are labradors, golden retrievers and standard poodles, although sometimes other large breeds are used. Guide dogs act as their owners' eyes and also keep them safe. Having a guide dog improves the quality of life for blind people by making them more independent and giving them more freedom.

Mobility issues Assistance dogs for people with mobility issues give their owners more freedom and independence. These dogs have special training to help their owners accomplish everyday tasks without help from other people. Dogs can help people dress and undress by pulling off items of clothing such as socks or jackets. They can retrieve items that their owners accidentally drop, such as a phone or a remote control. They can open doors, including the refrigerator door, which can be very difficult for someone with limited strength. Service dogs can also take an item from their owner and hand it to someone else. This is handy for shopping trips if the person doesn't have

enough control over their hands to count out money, or can't reach the counter to hand over a credit card.

Psychiatric issues

Of course, not all kinds of disabilities are visible, and assistance dogs can help people with mental illnesses and disabilities as well as those with physical limitations. Psychiatric service dogs are relatively new, and their owners still struggle for recognition. For people living with a serious mental illness, however, having an assistance dog trained to meet their needs can be extremely comforting and may even save lives. The duties of psychiatric service dogs are very personalized because symptoms of mental illness are so different

Ann and her assistance dog, Rosa.

from one person to another. In fact, unlike other assistance dogs, it's usually recommended that the owner of a psychiatric service dog participate in their training from the very beginning to create a strong bond and help the dog to recognize the owner's symptoms and behaviours.

These dogs help their owners by looking for clues. Some of the symptoms dogs can be trained to recognize include a racing heartbeat that might indicate a panic attack, compulsive behaviour such as pacing back and forth, becoming catatonic or unresponsive, having night terrors or showing nervousness by trembling or sweating. If the owner becomes confused or disoriented, the dog can take him or her to a safe place. If the owner is upset, scared or agitated, the dog can use touch to refocus and calm him or her. The dogs can also be trained to notice if their owners have forgotten to take their medication, and remind them by indicating the location of the medication. The world of mental illness can be a frightening place, but a well-trained assistance dog can make it a little bit easier to cope.

FOLLOW ME TO SAFETY

Alex Anderson was born with a visual impairment that got worse with age. By the time she reached her forties, Alex was living on her own in Edmonton, Alberta and decided she was ready to take on the responsibility of a guide dog. Her first dog, Clifford, was a standard poodle – perfect for someone like Alex who has allergies, because poodles don't shed much fur.

Clifford transformed Alex's life. Suddenly there was nowhere she couldn't go. Clifford made her feel safe and gave her companionship. He walked her to work and back. He even expanded her social life because more people would come up and talk to her to ask about her dog.

One evening when she was in her 14th floor apartment, the fire alarm sounded and everyone was told to evacuate the building. Out in the hallway, Clifford started guiding Alex to the elevators as usual, but the elevators couldn't be used during a fire alarm. Alex asked her neighbour for directions to the emergency stairs. Although the hallway was dark, Clifford was able to understand the neighbour's instructions and navigate Alex safely down the hall and into the stairwell.

The stairwells were dark, and people were having trouble finding their way around. For Alex and Clifford, however, the dark was not a problem. Realizing

Standard poodles have dense, hypoallergenic fur which is not shed as much as that of other dogs and, as in the case of Clifford, they make very loyal companions (and good rescuers).

that others were having trouble, Alex told people to lay a hand on the shoulder of the person in front of them, creating a human chain that began with Alex and Clifford. Her simple instruction to him was 'go boy' and he took the lead. As people descended from the floors above, Clifford safely led everyone coming from the 14th to 18th floors out of the building. It might have been an impressive feat to everyone who followed him down the stairs, but to Clifford it was all in a day's work.

DID YOU KNOW?

In many countries, people with assistance dogs have a legal right to keep their dogs with them in most places where the public is allowed, such as shops, restaurants, schools and workplaces. In the United Kingdom, these rights are protected under the Equality Act. In the US, the Americans with Disabilities Act protects the rights of people with service dogs and in Australia they're protected under the Disability Discrimination Act. Similar laws are in place in Japan and New Zealand. In Canada, each province and territory has its own laws regarding the rights of people with disabilities, but they are protected in every part of the country.

Unfortunately, some people have taken advantage of these protections by pretending that their pet dogs are assistance dogs. They dress the dogs in vests that look like assistant-dog vests and insist that the dog is allowed to be with them at all times. This has led to problems for people with legitimate assistance animals, because a lot of store and restaurant owners aren't sure who to believe. It's a shame that some people can be so thoughtless about how their actions affect others.

A labrador wearing his assistant-dog
vest, alongside his owner.

MEDICAL MARVELS

Pets are great to have around when we're sick. They offer us company, sympathy and comfort. But does your pet ever seem to know that you're sick or hurt even before you know? There are a lot of people who say their pets have a sixth sense that tells them when their owner is going to be in pain, have a seizure or experience other symptoms before they happen. So what do our animals know that we don't?

You might also ask 'Why should our pets care?' What does a pet hope to gain by letting a human know that he or she is sick? Some would argue that they see us as leading members of the pack, and so naturally wish to protect and support us. But the answer to this could also be evolutionary. We've been living side-by-side with dogs and cats for thousands of years. They have come to depend on their human companions for food, shelter and protection, as well as having an emotional connection. Losing their human could spell disaster for a pet. Without their owners, pets can find themselves abandoned and starving, not to mention lonely and grieving. So it's in their best interest to keep their favourite people safe and healthy. If they notice something amiss, they let us know. It's their way of saying, 'Maybe you should get that checked out!'

Can medical professionals learn to mimic our pets' uncanny abilities to help them diagnose our illnesses or foresee when symptoms will affect us? Research has begun to unravel the mysteries associated with animals that detect and predict health problems. While some of the findings have led to reliable training methods that help people with conditions such as diabetes or epilepsy manage their health, there are still some animal medical talents that we don't fully understand.

AVOIDING DIABETIC DISASTERS

Diabetes is the body's inability to regulate the amount of glucose in the bloodstream. In some cases (Type 1) people are born without the ability to produce the hormone insulin, which is needed for this regulation. In other cases (Type 2) people become less responsive to insulin and eventually their bodies lose the ability to self-regulate. In both cases, it's important for people with the condition to monitor their level of blood glucose and to respond to dangerous highs or lows by using medication, injecting insulin to bring down a high glucose level or eating something sugary to raise a low glucose level.

One of the most annoying aspects of having diabetes is the need to use blood glucose meters to check levels frequently. It's a process that involves pricking a finger to obtain a drop of blood that can be tested using a small machine. So the idea of having a back-up method monitoring your glucose levels has a lot of appeal. That's where diabetic alert dogs come in.

The idea behind diabetic alert dogs developed by accident. A few dog owners with diabetes noticed that whenever their dog behaved in a particular, strange way, it turned out that their blood glucose level was too high or too low. The dog would most often whine or paw at them. It usually took some time before the owner made the connection between the dog's behaviour and their diabetes, but once the connection was made they could use this warning system to help them stay healthier and avoid dangerous drops or peaks in their blood glucose.

Researchers heard about these anecdotes, which were common enough to make them think that when owners had a problem with their glucose levels,

The 12-year-old twins Jade and Brooke Bordman with their service dog, Nettle, at the annual Purina Animal Hall of Fame induction ceremony in 2015. Both girls have Type 1 diabetes and coeliac disease and Nettle is able to alert their parents whenever their blood sugar falls out of range. Nettle is one of the first diabetic alert dogs to be trained at Lions Foundation of Canada Dog Guides.

something changed that the dogs could detect. Eventually they determined that chemical changes in the body meant that the dogs could smell the problem on their owners' breath.

Dogs can now be specifically trained to recognize this smell and respond to it. With children, the dog can be trained to alert a parent or teacher so that the child can be given insulin or a snack as needed. For adults, the warning could be a simple alert bark or nudge, or it could be a more specific task such as fetching a diabetic kit with medication and/or a glucose meter.

Diabetic alert dogs are not 100 per cent accurate. Sometimes they don't notice the change in blood glucose if it isn't severe. Sometimes they might give a false alarm. But for their owners, they provide extra help in fighting this life-threatening disease. In one study, 60 per cent of people with diabetic alert dogs said they were less worried about episodes of high or low blood glucose than they were before getting the dogs. Three-quarters of the study participants reported that the dogs improved their ability to participate in physical activities, which is an important factor in managing Type 2 diabetes. Three-quarters of the participants also reported a general improvement in their quality of life.

PREDICTING SEIZURES

Epilepsy is a chronic condition marked by sudden seizures, putting the person with the condition in potential danger. Managing this condition can be a struggle, especially when the seizures happen without warning. They can also be frightening and disorienting.

As with diabetic alert dogs, the idea that dogs could be helpful to people with epilepsy emerged from the personal experiences of dog owners. Some people realized that their dogs helped to protect them during and after a seizure by standing guard or comforting them. Others noticed that their dogs would behave strangely before a seizure even started, leading them to believe that their dogs could predict when the seizures were coming.

Not all dogs can be trained to help owners with epilepsy. After all, a seizure can be very frightening for a dog, who may not understand what has happened to their owner. Some dogs' instincts tell them to run away when this happens. Others become aggressive to anyone who approaches to help because they are trying to protect their owner. But many dogs can be trained to help people with epilepsy, giving them a better, safer life.

Seizure response dogs are trained to recognize when their owner is having a seizure, and to perform certain tasks. These tasks can include standing guard to keep their owner out of danger, placing themselves in a position to break their owner's fall, pressing an alarm button or alerting a designated person when a seizure begins and helping their owner to move to a safe place at the start or end of a seizure. The dogs can also carry important emergency information or even medication in a vest or backpack, so that when help arrives their owner gets assistance right away.

Ideally, a dog can be trained to alert their owner well before a seizure even begins. This allows the owner to get to a safe place, put down anything they are carrying or even get home before anything happens. Training a dog to alert its owner before a seizure can be difficult, so even professional trainers who specialize in these dogs can't guarantee that every dog will be able to learn this skill. Some associations for people with epilepsy warn that the dogs shouldn't be relied on, and to be dubious of any unrealistic promises made by trainers, especially if they are asking for a lot of money to train a dog.

On the other hand, many people with epilepsy have dogs that do alert them ahead of a seizure, giving them a warning anywhere between 30 seconds and 45 minutes in advance. (Once a dog starts alerting its owner a certain time before the seizure, there's usually about the same warning period every time.) This can make a huge difference to the owner's personal safety. It can also provide a lot of independence to someone who otherwise depends on family and friends to be around in case they have a seizure. Epilepsy is different for each person, so some people can live basically normal lives with the condition, while others find it difficult to feel confident about their safety or how people will perceive them. For some people with epilepsy, getting an alert dog makes doing things that most of us take for granted – such as shopping or taking the bus to work on their own – worry-free for the first time. Training a seizure response or alert dog can take anywhere from six months to two years.

But how can a dog possibly predict when their owner is going to have a seizure? Part of the reason only some people can count on an alert dog may have more to do with the person than their dog. Seizures can manifest in different ways, with different symptoms. Some people get migraines with seizures, others see auras, get dizzy or lightheaded, feel nauseated or just get a weird feeling in their heads. Some of these symptoms may start in subtle ways long before the actual seizure begins. When dogs are trained by getting a reward when they react properly to a seizure, the dogs will also start to look for patterns and clues that tell them when a seizure is likely to happen. These clues may be so subtle that the person experiencing them isn't even aware of them. Slight changes in body posture or tell-tale hand gestures, for example, could tip off a dog that a seizure is coming soon. This is a good theory for how dogs learn to predict seizures in their owners.

On the other hand, there is anecdotal evidence that some dogs can detect an oncoming seizure even when they are not in the same room as their owner. Although it is possible that there's a psychic connection between dogs and owners, this behaviour could also suggest that there's something more than body language at work. It's credible that there are changes in body chemistry leading up to a seizure, such as the release of certain hormones. In this case, the dog might actually be able to smell a seizure coming.

Both diabetic alert dogs and seizure response dogs are considered assistance animals; this means that their owners should be allowed to take them along to places where pets are not normally allowed, such as offices, restaurants and shops. Anywhere you can bring a guide dog you can bring a diabetic alert or epilepsy response dog. Unfortunately, these roles for service dogs are not as well known and it's impossible to tell at first sight whether someone has diabetes or epilepsy. People with these types of service dogs are often challenged by staff at various places and told their dogs aren't allowed in. Hopefully, with more public education, people with all types of assistance dogs will have their rights respected.

CANCER STINKS!

Early detection can greatly increase your chances of surviving cancer, but by the time symptoms appear and an official diagnosis is confirmed, the cancer has often progressed beyond the earliest stages. Any new tool that can detect cancers sooner would greatly reduce the number of lives lost to this widespread disease. So, how can dogs help?

It turns out that dogs can be trained to recognize the smell of some kinds of cancer, even before there are any symptoms that the patient can detect. It may seem strange to you that cancer has a recognizable smell, but it's actually no surprise to oncologists (cancer specialists) who say that in the late stages of the disease, even humans notice a distinct smell on the breath of cancer patients. Dogs, however, have a sense of smell thousands of times more sensitive than ours, so they can smell it much sooner.

Cancer is such a common and deadly disease that researchers are willing to explore any avenue to save more lives. Studies on dogs' abilities to sniff out cancer have had promising results. Studies involving samples of breath, urine and biopsies of affected areas have shown that dogs can definitely smell which samples are from patients with cancer and which are not. These studies involved dogs sniffing four or five samples and choosing the correct ones. Much like training dogs to identify the smell of narcotics or explosives, by rewarding the dogs' successes their handlers were able to train them to indicate when they found a cancer sample.

While there is no doubt that dogs can identify the smell of a particular type of cancer when trained to do so, the reliability of their skills is not strong enough to screen for cancer this way. In the studies, there were too many false positive and false negative indications for researchers to feel confident that dogs are ready to save the day.

This research is not a waste, however, as scientists are taking what they've learned from the dogs and applying it to a different approach. Scientists at the Israel Institute of Technology are working on developing 'sniffer' machines that detect the same subtle components in the breath or urine of sick patients that dogs are able to smell. Some recent research was conducted with a machine using carbon nanotubes and gold particles to isolate chemicals called volatile organic compounds in samples of exhaled breath from over 1,400 participants. The machine was programmed to recognize the chemical signatures associated with 17 different diseases, including cancers, Crohn's disease and Parkinson's disease. The machine identified the diseases each participant had with 86 per cent accuracy. Scientists around the world are working on similar cancer-spotting breath analysers, including one group at Imperial College, London, and another team, looking specifically at lung cancer, at the University of Leicester.

The best part of this new technology is the price. These machines can be manufactured for around £25 each – much less than the cost of training a cancer-sniffing dog. So we may not find a dog at the doctor's office any time soon to help diagnose disease, but we can thank the dogs that participated in these studies for helping researchers, oncologists and engineers to build a better mechanical nose.

NURSE KITTY

We've been giving dogs a lot of credit for looking after their people, but what about cats? Cats have a reputation for being self-centred and not caring much about what their owners are up to, but that reputation is not entirely deserved. Cats can certainly be affectionate and devoted to their owners, and as we're about to see, they can also be excellent caregivers.

While there hasn't been significant research into the abilities of cats to identify illnesses or injuries in humans, there is certainly lots of anecdotal evidence that they possess talents in this area. One of the most common stories cat owners share about this comes from people who regularly suffer from migraines. These debilitating headaches can cause severe pain and nausea that

Cats have been known to detect migraines and blood glucose levels. They may even attempt to relieve symptoms by using their paws to massage, or knead, their owners.

lasts for hours. For many people, the key to avoiding the worst effects is taking their medication at the earliest sign of an oncoming migraine. Spotting the symptoms early, and taking quick action, reduces the severity and duration of the attacks.

Cats have been known to show concern for their owners before they begin to feel the onset of a migraine. They might do this by lying on or against their owner's head. If that's not possible, they may indicate it in another way, by meowing or pawing at the owner, for example. Some owners say that their cat massages their head during a migraine, and seems to know exactly where the pain is worst.

How can a cat tell when a migraine is coming? It is likely that the cat has noticed some changes taking place in their owner's behaviour. Some symptoms that can precede a migraine include dizziness, irritability, hyperactivity, neck pain, yawning and frequent urination. If a cat spots the connection between a certain behaviour in their owner (like rubbing his or her neck or yawning frequently) and the migraine that occurs later, they might start reacting to those symptoms. This is all speculation though, because there have been no scientific studies to determine whether this is how cats recognize migraines.

Cats have also been known to alert owners with diabetes when their blood glucose is dangerously low. Although cats don't seem to be trainable to do this, some owners credit their cats with saving their lives or the lives of their children. From the stories that have been reported in the media, it seems as if they only notice the low blood glucose when it becomes extreme. Whether they smell it, as dogs do, or have another method of recognizing it, is a question that remains to be answered.

Cat owners also report in many cases that their cats can tell when they are in pain, and where the pain is located. The cats will lie against the painful area or massage it with their paws. One possible explanation for this is that pain is often caused by inflammation, which gives off heat. The cats could be sensing the warmth radiating from the injured or painful area and targeting it that way. After all, cats love finding the warmest place to curl up for a nap. Again, there haven't been any studies to show how cats know where their owners are hurting, but they certainly do seem to be able to tell where the pain is coming from.

COACH ON THE COUCH

Laurie and Bryan own a shih tzu named Thomson. Thomson is more Bryan's dog than Laurie's, and doesn't generally pay much attention to Laurie at all. But something interesting started to happen after she was diagnosed with Type 2 diabetes.

Thomson, the clever shih tzu with an uncanny ability to monitor the blood glucose level of his owner, Laurie.

The first incident happened on Easter Sunday at the family's traditional holiday brunch. Before eating, Laurie checked her blood glucose and administered an insulin injection as usual at mealtimes. After brunch, Thomson, who generally ignored Laurie, wouldn't leave her alone. He was whimpering and climbed up onto her lap, pushing himself against her. Laurie put him back on the floor time and time again. He simply kept jumping back up. Then he started to lick her face. Bryan touched her arm and told her that she felt slightly clammy. That was one of her indicators of low blood sugar so she decided to check her level. It was severely low, and oddly enough the dog stopped bothering her after she corrected the problem.

The following year, Laurie decided to take up running and put a treadmill behind the couch in the living room. One day, Thomson climbed on the back of the couch and started whimpering. When she ignored him, he started pacing and growling, then barked at her. Frustrated, Laurie got off the treadmill and let him outside. He wanted to come back in immediately and the odd behaviour continued. She checked that he had fresh water and food then headed back to the treadmill. There he was, up on the back of the couch again! Laurie cut the workout short and checked her blood sugar like she always did after a run. It was very low and had she continued running that day it could have been dangerous. Laurie then made the connection that Thomson could sense when her blood glucose levels were dropping.

As Laurie's diabetes progressed, her ability to sense the lows diminished significantly. Thomson's uncanny ability to tell when Laurie was about to go into the danger zone was a gift and it strengthened their bond. To this day, you'll find Thomson protectively lying in wait on the back of the couch while Laurie runs.

DID YOU KNOW?

Not only can cats sometimes spot pain, they may also be able to help relieve it with a simple purr. A 1983 study on chronic pain found that applying vibratory stimulation to the area helped to reduce pain. The ideal frequency for these vibrations was found to be 50–150 Hz. It just so happens that this is the frequency at which cats purr!

The only catch is that you'll need to hold a purring cat against the area that's in pain for at least 30 minutes to enjoy the relieving effects. While some cats would be happy to oblige (especially if it's your lap that happens to be in pain) it would be difficult to count on this solution. In the study, which used a machine to produce the vibrations, some of the participants found that after 30 minutes of treatment the pain relief lasted for 3 hours or longer and, in some cases, up to 12 hours.

At this stage, nobody has repeated this experiment using cats. As you can imagine, getting a large number of cats to purr on cue for long periods of time would be challenging, if not impossible. But cat owners may want to try out this theory on pain relief for themselves and discover whether their cats can purr the pain away.

THERAPY ON FOUR LEGS

Can a dog help children learn to read or a dolphin improve the life of a wounded war veteran? Can a horse help someone with autism to communicate or a cat revive the mind of a grandmother with Alzheimer's disease? It seems like a lot to ask from an animal, but more and more experts are convinced that they can do all of these things and more.

Therapy animals are a relatively recent development. A few decades ago, no respectable hospital would have let a dog through its doors, let alone have them visit patients and sit on their beds. But as more evidence accumulates for the positive effects of interacting with therapy animals, the medical community is including them more often as part of their treatment programmes. Some animals seem to have a natural instinct that tells them who needs their help. They will walk through a room and sit beside the person who is feeling stressed or upset in order to comfort them. Not every animal has this talent, of course, but those who do are providing all kinds of benefits to people with a huge range of physical and psychological conditions. Therapy animals may be a new phenomenon in an official capacity, but animals have been used in therapeutic settings since the 17th century by medical experts including Sigmund Freud.

A therapy dog visits a patient in hospital.

RETRIEVING FOND MEMORIES

The modern therapy animal movement began with people bringing dogs into nursing homes to interact with the elderly residents. The results were amazing. Residents who were remote and unresponsive when surrounded by people responded to the dogs, smiling and stroking their fur. People with almost no mobility made an effort to pick up a ball dropped in their lap and throw it for the dog to fetch. Some who seemed to have completely lost their memory due to Alzheimer's disease or other forms of dementia began to reminisce about the dogs they had as children. Residents who were angry and disruptive calmed down so that they wouldn't upset the dog.

Cats have also been used as therapy animals for older people. After all, not everyone is a dog person and some residents react more powerfully to stroking a cat. For people who were cat owners earlier in life, and were perhaps forced to give up owning cats when they could no longer stay in their own homes, visits from a therapy cat can provide company, comfort and fond memories. For a cat to become an effective therapy animal it has to be affectionate and willing to be handled by anyone. It can't be frightened by dogs, loud noises or other activities in the home. If a resident hasn't had a visit from friends or family for a while, a purring cat on their lap can be a very welcome diversion. And if there is an ongoing programme of animal visits in their residence, it can give them something to look forward to.

REACHING OUT

The use of therapy animals has expanded over the years, extending to areas that you might not expect. For example, dogs are now used in some schools and libraries to help children who are falling behind their peers when it comes to reading. These include the dogs of the charity Pets as Therapy, which comes under the umbrella of the Kennel Club's Bark and Read Foundation. The children are paired with calm dogs (often from local shelters) and read aloud to the dogs. Having someone listen without judgment gives the children an opportunity to practise without feeling self-conscious about making a mistake. It's also good for the shelter dogs because they get to spend more time outside their kennels and learn to socialize with children, which makes them more adoptable. Everybody wins.

Therapy dogs have been used to help with a large number of conditions, including post-traumatic stress disorder (PTSD), depression, autism, attention deficit disorder (ADD), Down's Syndrome and physical disabilities. Scientific studies proving that therapy dogs benefit people with these conditions are lagging behind the anecdotal evidence, but there is some scientific proof of how it might work. For example, studies have shown that petting an animal releases hormones in our bodies that make us feel relaxed and happy. They are some of the same hormones that are released when we eat chocolate or when we fall in love. Studies have also shown that interacting with animals can lower blood pressure and reduce the level of stress hormones in the body. It's easy to see how these hormone responses would help people with depression or PTSD, as well as other psychological conditions.

Therapy dogs are also used in generally stressful situations, even when the people involved are not necessarily ill or disabled. After natural or man-made disasters, therapy dogs are often brought in to help people deal with their feelings and to calm them down. After disasters such as Hurricane Katrina in Louisiana or the bombing at the 2013 Boston Marathon, dogs and their volunteer handlers arrived to help people express their feelings and find a bit of joy in a furry cuddle. The dogs offered comfort and support to people dealing with the trauma of the disaster and also to disaster-relief workers who often feel as if there's nobody they can talk to about the horrors they have witnessed. People who are strong and brave in the face of death and destruction can benefit from having a dog lick their tears away when it becomes too much to bear.

Several universities have brought in puppies during exam time to help students relax, including Bristol and Aberdeen universities, which both teamed up with the Guide Dogs charity. Exam stress can be almost unbearable for some students, leading to serious mental health problems if they can't find a way to cope. Interacting with therapy dogs gives students a break and reduces levels of stress hormones. The dogs also lighten the tense atmosphere that can pervade a university campus during exam time.

Even airports have begun employing therapy dogs to ease the tension that comes with long queues, security checks, flight delays and lost luggage. The dogs roam the departures area with their handlers, accepting pats and cuddles from stressed-out travellers. They can also provide a distraction for children who are travelling with their families. Airports are boring for kids, and airlines insist on passengers arriving hours before their flight departs; a therapy dog is a welcome diversion. It's estimated that there are around 30 airports now using therapy dogs in the United States and at least half a dozen in Canada. There's even one pig on the job (see Did You Know, page 84). The trend for airport therapy animals, however, has yet to take off in Europe.

THERAPY IN ALL SHAPES AND SIZES

Dogs and cats are not the only animals that provide therapy. Horses are also popular therapists. This is nothing new: the ancient Greeks recognized the therapeutic benefits of riding, and in 1875 Charles Chassaignac, a French neurologist, found that riding improved balance and muscle control in patients with neurological disorders. After the First World War horses were used in Oxford for the rehabilitation of wounded soldiers. However, it is Lis Hartel of Denmark who is credited with being the spark for therapeutic riding as we now know it. Lis had been debilitated by polio but still won a silver medal for dressage in the 1952 Helsinki Olympics. Elsbet Bodtker, a Norwegian physiotherapist, met Lis and was inspired to give riding lessons to young patients. The rest, as they say, is history.

Horses are thought to be good therapy animals for people with psychological, neurological or intellectual disabilities because they are very sensitive and perceptive. They react to people's moods and behaviour, and sometimes seem to mirror what the rider is feeling. This can be helpful, for example, for people with severe autism. Autism can make it very difficult for some people to express their feelings or communicate with others. Horses, however, seem to understand and react in predictable ways that provide valuable feedback to people with this isolating condition.

Horses can also help people with intellectual disabilities to feel more powerful and independent. Having a huge animal like a horse respond to your commands is a remarkable feeling, particularly if you cannot control very much in your day-to-day life. Riding horses can help to build confidence in people who are constantly reminded of what they can't do. For children with intellectual or physical disabilities, riding therapy can be especially effective for improving their confidence and self-esteem.

Another therapy animal is the dolphin. Dolphins are known for their intelligence and their playful nature, which also makes them great therapists. Both children and adults can benefit from interacting with dolphins in the water. For people with physical disabilities, the water can provide them with an opportunity to do things that are impossible for them on land. Floating among playful dolphins can bring hope to people who are depressed or frustrated about their physical limitations.

However, there is another side to this. Dolphin therapy is uncommon because it calls for a number of dolphins to be kept in captivity and requires heavy supervision to keep everyone safe. It is also controversial because dolphins do not always do well in captivity, living shorter lives despite being in a protected environment. And while some dolphins may enjoy human interaction, they can also sometimes lash out, causing injury to themselves or the people they are with.

WHAT MAKES A GOOD THERAPY ANIMAL?

Therapy animals are different from assistance animals in several ways, but they also have similarities. Both need to be well behaved, social, non-aggressive and calm. As you can imagine, having an excitable dog running around a hospital ward full of frail patients and expensive equipment does not go down well. A good temperament and love of meeting new people are also essential.

Where therapy animals differ from assistance animals is in their training. Therapy animals don't necessarily have special training, although some organizations offer courses and certifications. They don't need to learn special skills or tasks – they just need to be themselves. For this reason, almost any breed of dog or cat can become a therapy animal. In fact, different kinds of animals are used in different situations. Sometimes small dogs are brought into nursing homes, for example, because they can sit on residents' laps and are

A 12-year-old disabled boy attends a therapeutic horse-riding session at the Army Service Corps Centre in Bangalore in 2009. Horse riding is believed to benefit cognitive, emotional, physical and social skills in children. Equine therapist Pushpa Bopaiah believes that the rhythmic movement of the horse is similar to the human gait and the heat of the animal's body acts as physiotherapy for stiff muscles in disabled children.

unlikely to scare anyone. In some cases, a vest is worn by therapy dogs so that they are easy to identify. The vests will often say something like 'pet me' to let people know that it's okay to approach the dogs.

The laws about dogs also recognize a difference between assistance dogs and therapy dogs. While assistance dogs are allowed to go almost anywhere with their owners (such as schools, shops, restaurants and workplaces) therapy dogs are not automatically allowed in places where pet dogs can't go. It's up to the individual business or institution whether they will allow therapy animals in. Thankfully, lots of schools, hospitals, nursing homes and other places have begun to recognize the benefits of these animals and are allowing them to come in and help their students, patients and residents.

GETTING BACK ON HER FEET

Hollie owns two miniature poodles, Stevie and Emmet, who both volunteer as therapy dogs. Hollie takes Stevie to visit young patients at Toronto's Sick Kids Hospital every week.

One day Hollie took Stevie into the room of a little girl about four years old – we'll call her Anne. Anne's mother had stepped out to get a coffee, but Anne said she was happy to have a visit from Stevie. Hollie offered to put Stevie up on the bed with her, but Anne said that it was fine to leave him on the floor.

Over the next few minutes, Anne slid herself off the bed to sit on the floor next to Stevie. Anne's mother returned and was shocked to see her out of bed. For the last week, Anne had refused to leave her bed, even though her mother and the hospital staff had been trying to convince her to get up.

Hollie saw the opportunity for Stevie to help Anne even more. 'Would you like to take Stevie for a walk?' she asked Anne. Anne agreed to walk Stevie down the hallway. Not only had she left her bed for the first time in a week, she was now walking around, much to her mother's delight.

Sometimes people just need to be distracted by something positive, so that they forget about what they 'can't' do or don't want to do, and focus on enjoying the company of a beautiful, new friend like Stevie the miniature poodle.

In addition to convincing Anne to leave her bed, Stevie has encouraged elderly people to throw a ball for her and play fetch, given a man permission to cry

Stevie the miniature poodle with one of her friends.

because he missed his own dogs while in hospital and encouraged a diabetic child to attend her educational clinic because she knew that she would get to play with Stevie while she was there. Hollie says that visiting people with her therapy dogs is the most rewarding volunteer work she's ever done.

DID YOU KNOW?

Sometimes a therapy animal can make a difference simply by surprising people. At the San Francisco Airport, there was already a programme in place for using therapy dogs to help passengers relax. But in 2016, LiLou the Juliana pig made her debut as a certified therapy animal at the airport. The Juliana pig is a miniature breed and, like all pigs, they are clever and sociable. LiLou, for example, likes to cuddle and knows how to do a few tricks to entertain her admirers. She is also happy to get dressed up in costumes, in case the sight of a pig in the airport wasn't amusing enough. She has a collection of tutus and even wears hats – including everything from a Mexican sombrero to a pilot's cap.

Juliana pigs, or miniature painted pigs, are a breed of small and colourful pigs that are known for their curiosity, inquisitiveness and intelligence.

ARE YOU MY MOTHER?

Every once in a while we hear a story about an animal that has adopted young from a different species. It seems like a strange thing for animals to do, especially if they are taking care of creatures that they might normally eat! It's a mysterious behaviour that has been observed in a variety of creatures. It seems to happen most often with domesticated animals such as dogs, but it does happen in the wild too.

It is certainly not uncommon for birds to sit on another bird's eggs. We've all heard of the *Ugly Duckling* story, in which a swan's egg was hatched by a duck. Likewise, a broody hen will happily step off the nest in the early stages for another hen to lay her eggs and then immediately return to it. So strong is a hen's brooding instinct, that she will also hatch duck, guinea fowl and other eggs if the poultry-keeper is able to slip them in – and she'll raise the chicks too. Particularly fascinating is the story of the great tinamou from South America. These birds live in groups, and the females lay their bright turquoise eggs in shared nest sites. Then it's over to the males, who take on the dangerous job of incubating the eggs in each nest alone, even though they may not have fertilized a single one themselves.

Hatching another bird's egg is one thing, but what about live young? In this case it must be pretty obvious that the young belong somewhere else. There are some theories about this behaviour and why it might happen, even though it seems to go against the evolutionary directive of only caring for your own young. If the orphaned or abandoned baby is from the same species, the phenomenon is not so strange. This adoption of a baby from an animal's own species is what scientists call 'kin selection'. Mother animals are genetically hard-wired to care for youngsters of their own kind because the additional family members will help to protect their own young and enhance the status of the family. They might also contribute to family duties such as hunting and caring for the next generation to come, depending on the species.

Indeed, in some species, parenting is habitually shared, with all the mothers helping to raise all the young. In this case, you would expect adoption to be common if a mother dies before her offspring are old enough to survive on their own. But is adoption always a generous act? When does adoption become kidnapping? Not all animals raised by adults who aren't their parents are orphans. In certain species, adult couples without their own offspring (or whose offspring have died) sometimes kidnap babies from other parents and raise them as their own. This has been known to happen among penguins, for example. Sadly, the kidnapped penguin chicks are often abandoned by their new parents in a week or less. Kidnapping behaviour has also been studied in other animals such as mongooses and certain bird species, including black swans. It is thought that when animals live in large co-operative groups, it can be beneficial to the group to add more members even if it means stealing them from another group.

Adoption has also been observed among elephant seals on Ano Nuevo Island off the coast of California. The crowded beaches and heavy surf mean that sometimes young seal pups get separated from their mothers. When this happens, another seal might step in and become a foster parent to the pup. Only adult females appear to help the lost pups, which makes sense since the pups need to nurse.

An emperor penguin with chick. Penguins have been known to practise adoption of young, and even to kidnap the offspring of others.

Researchers observed the seal population over several breeding seasons to find out more about their behaviour. They found that the most likely seals to adopt a pup were mother seals whose own pups had died. They thought that perhaps raising another pup helped the females to stay fertile for the next mating season because nursing a pup can induce ovulation. They also observed that some of the pups were adopted by females that hadn't had any pups of their own yet. The theory as to why this happened was that it offered them valuable practice at parenting to improve their skills before raising their own young. Of course, these are just theories since it's difficult to get seals to explain their reasoning, but the fact remains that adoption was common on the island for one reason or another.

Things get more complicated, however, when the baby animal is a different species from the mother. What good is it for a dog to nurse a baby squirrel instead of hunting it? Perhaps if the dog has been nursing her own pups, the maternal instinct fuelled by her hormones is so strong that it extends to all hungry babies. The hormone oxytocin, which is sometimes called the bonding hormone, is produced in new mothers to help them create a strong attachment to their young. If an animal already producing this bonding hormone is presented with a new baby, she might feel a connection to the baby, even if it is from another species, and take care of it.

Researchers in Canada tested another theory for why cross-species adoptions might occur. They suspected that because the distress cries of baby mammals are all quite similar, they provoke a response in adult mammals of any species. Basically, they were testing whether the cry of a baby in trouble was so compelling that adult animals were moved to care for the troubled babies even though they weren't the same species. They tested their theory using two species of deer and found that they did respond to the cries of several baby mammals, but not to the cries of predators or to non-animal sounds in the same frequency range. Among the mammal cries they tested were marmots, seals, domestic cats, bats and even humans. While this only proves the theory as far as deer are concerned, it does provide some insight and perhaps further studies will confirm that other animals behave the same way. Certainly, humans have

been known to respond when they hear baby animals cry. The whimpering of a puppy, the soft mews of a hungry kitten or the cheeps of a baby bird can tug at our heartstrings. Perhaps other animals are not so different from us.

Adopting or foster parenting between species is not a sure thing by any means. Most animals will reject (or eat) a baby animal from another species that they find alone and unprotected. But it does happen, and it can be quite heart-warming to witness the selflessness of some animals that reach out to those in need, in defiance of their usual instincts.

WHO'S RAISING WHOM?

There are all kinds of animals that have been cared for by adoptive parents, no doubt saving their young lives. Dogs are known to make good mothers to other species, especially when they are already nursing pups of their own, or have just weaned them but are still producing milk. There are some dogs, however, who have started producing milk when presented with a baby to nurse even though they weren't nursing at the time. Dogs have nursed all kinds of animals including kittens and baby squirrels. It's hard to imagine, but a pit bull terrier once adopted three baby turkeys and took care of them.

In Cuba, one dog became a minor celebrity when she started nursing a whole litter of piglets. The owner wasn't sure what to do when the piglets' mother died, but thought it was worth trying to get his dog to raise them. The dog was nursing her own litter of six puppies already, and was hesitant to take on further nursing duties at first. But within a week she was providing milk to the piglets, even seeking them out to nurse them. When the story made local news, people started coming by to see the generous dog and her piglet children.

Another story that made headlines involved the owners of a safari park in the United States whose white Bengal tiger had three cubs, but rejected them and refused to nurse them. The owners brought the newborn cubs to their home and introduced them to their golden retriever. She adopted the cubs and nursed them. Once they were big enough, the cubs were moved back to the safari park, where they live today.

Cats have also taken on inter-species parenting duties. A cat in the UK even adopted a rabbit. The rabbit's mother had died, which would normally be a death sentence for the youngster, especially when faced with a predator such as a cat. But instead of attacking the helpless rabbit, the cat decided to take on parenting duties.

Domestic cats are not the only ones who have put aside their hunting instincts to show their more nurturing side. In one amazing event, a leopard killed a baboon and then saw that there was a baby baboon clinging to the dead mother. Instead of killing the baby as well, the leopard stopped to comfort the orphan. In another strange situation, a lioness at a reserve in Kenya adopted orphaned oryx calves, not just once but an incredible six times during her life. An oryx is an antelope – exactly the kind of animal that lions normally hunt.

Apes and orangutans have also shown themselves to be excellent foster parents. They have cared for babies from all kinds of species, including puppies and kittens. This happens most often with apes that have been raised in captivity. Perhaps this is because they aren't worried about their own survival like apes would be in the wild. Knowing that they are safe and food is plentiful, they have the luxury of caring for pets much like humans do. Studies have proved that primates do feel empathy, and this would explain why they are interested in helpless baby animals of different species.

SHELTER DOG SHELTERS KITTENS

It's not unusual for an animal shelter such as the Humane Society to end up with a litter of newborn puppies or kittens to care for. Often, these animals are found abandoned by pet owners who didn't want to take care of them. At other times, the mother of the litter has died or has rejected her babies for some reason.

A newborn litter is a lot of work for a shelter. The young need to be fed by bottle several times a day, around the clock. It takes a team of very dedicated volunteers to care for them until they are old enough to be weaned and eventually adopted to new homes. But sometimes the shelter can make things easier by finding a foster parent for the litter. If they happen to have a dog or

A young orangutan shows affection for a cat in Tanjung Puting National Park, Borneo.

A labrador and kitten. As in the case of Lily, labradors have been known to act as foster parents to the young of other species.

cat in the shelter who recently had a litter of her own, she might be willing to nurse the new litter, too, much to the relief of the human volunteers.

That's what happened at the Des Moines County Humane Society in Iowa a few years ago. The shelter took in a pregnant labrador cross who was found by the side of the road. They decided to name her Lily. While living at the shelter, Lily gave birth to her litter of six puppies, caring for them until they were old enough to be adopted.

Soon the shelter was in a predicament. Someone dropped off a litter of tiny kittens with no mother. They placed their hopes in Lily, but weren't sure how she would react to the kittens. Lily, however, instantly took to her new role as mother cat. She nursed the kittens until they too were old enough to find new homes.

DID YOU KNOW?

Different mammals need to nurse from their mothers for different lengths of time. Generally, the bigger the animal the longer it spends nursing. For example, mice can be weaned after four weeks of nursing, while young elephants need to nurse from their mothers for at least two years, and sometimes nurse for up to four years.

A ring-tailed lemur nursing its baby.

There are also differences between small domestic animals and their larger wild cousins. Kittens can be weaned after six to eight weeks. Tiger cubs, on the other hand, nurse for at least three months. Puppies and wolves nurse for similar lengths of time (around seven weeks) but wolves begin eating regurgitated food brought back by the adults in the pack very soon after birth. Domestic puppies can start eating solid food along with their mother's milk at around three or four weeks old.

Those first weeks of life, when baby animals are completely dependent on their mothers' milk, are the most difficult to get through for orphaned or abandoned animals. In many cases, being adopted by other animals or rescued by humans is their only hope for survival.

FURRY FORECASTERS

When a large natural disaster strikes, you can be sure that after the initial headlines have run their course, someone will proclaim that the local animals saw it coming. There are countless stories about pets behaving strangely before an earthquake or other disaster, farm animals getting agitated and trying to flee and wildlife heading for the hills. Do animals have a sixth sense that tells them when something terrible is about to happen? Or are we just attributing coincidences to an ability that isn't really there? There are billions of animals in the world; surely lots of them are behaving strangely at any given moment in time. However, if animals really can predict natural disasters such as earthquakes, shouldn't we be watching their behaviour more carefully so that we can prepare ourselves before disaster strikes?

The benefits of getting a head start on preparations for unpredictable weather disasters would be enormous and life-saving. That's why scientists have been interested in these stories of animal weather prediction for a long time. They want to know whether we can rely on animal behaviour to tip us off, and how much advance warning they can give us. If the animals can sense an earthquake or tsunami on the way, how are they doing it? Can we design equipment that does the same thing? Researchers have been looking into these questions and more.

DID YOU FEEL THE EARTH MOVE?

Earthquakes can be both terrifying and incredibly destructive: buildings collapse, roads split apart, power lines topple and people panic as the ground rocks under their feet. It's no surprise that animals are distressed by them, too. But can they really tell that an earthquake is coming before it starts?

The stories of animals predicting earthquakes go back further than you might imagine. The earliest recorded reference dates to 373BC in Greece, when rats, weasels, snakes and centipedes were observed fleeing their homes several days before a destructive earthquake. Since then, there have been many similar stories about fish, farm animals, pets, vermin and insects. Some animals have been observed behaving strangely days or weeks ahead of an earthquake, while others have changed their behaviour just hours or minutes before the disaster.

One American study used historical events to see if a real connection could be made between the behaviour of dogs and the onset of earthquakes in California, which sits on a fault line, meaning that earthquakes happen quite frequently. Since the most common reaction of a dog to an earthquake is to flee (probably due to the same fight or flight response that humans feel when something frightening happens) the researchers decided to look at dates when earthquakes had hit the area. They then analysed the lost pets section of the local newspaper to see whether a larger than usual number of dogs seemed to run away in the days leading up to an earthquake, as some people had claimed was the case. They looked at data for a three-year period and found that there was no significant evidence that dogs ran away more often when an earthquake was about to happen.

A 2011 report that was undertaken by the International College of Economics and Finance (ICEF) on the effectiveness of using animal behaviour as a predictor for earthquakes also came to the conclusion that there was no compelling evidence that animals could reliably predict earthquakes.

Despite the lack of evidence, at least one city in China – Nanchang – has been keeping dogs at its earthquake bureau since 2013 to provide an early warning.

A couple of mice emerge from their underground home. This behaviour can sometimes be a sign of an imminent earthquake, as changes in ground-water force the rodents to surface.

Scientists may not have proof that animals can predict earthquakes but there are certain events that can be connected with an upcoming earthquake that we might be able to observe through animal behaviour. For example, seismic activity in the area can cause changes in the ground-water level, so animals that live underground, such as earthworms and mice, will leave their homes as the water starts to fill them.

Also, the initial stage of an earthquake's movement, called a P wave, is too small for humans to feel. But some animals can feel the P wave and react to the earthquake before a person standing right next to them knows that it has begun. There may be other signs of the coming earthquake that we can't detect, such as disturbances in the Earth's electromagnetic fields. This kind of disturbance could be felt by animals that use the fields as navigation aids. This would affect cats, birds and other animals. Could electromagnetic changes be tipping them off about an upcoming earthquake? Even if they didn't know what the changes meant, they would be upset and agitated by the unexplained change.

Some animals are also very sensitive to other small changes including tilt, humidity and air pressure. If an animal detects these kinds of changes and can't attribute them to anything it understands, the animal might conclude that something is wrong and react accordingly.

Another possibility is that the animals can hear the sounds of the coming earthquake before humans can see, hear or feel anything. Many animals have hearing that is far superior to ours, so they could certainly hear low rumbling noises underground that would not be audible to us.

One researcher based in California proposed that animals might even have evolved in some parts of the world to connect these tiny changes with earthquakes. He believed that over generations, animals that were aware of the dangers connected with earthquakes (broken eggs, destruction of dens or nests, falling debris, etc.) had a much better chance of surviving them and passing along their extra-cautious genes.

Although it seems reasonable that some animals can tell when an earthquake is on the way, most of these possible signs do not occur far enough in advance for the warning to be terribly useful to humans. It might give someone who is directly observing the animal time to get to a safer place, but there would probably not be enough warning to evacuate cities or close bridges to traffic in the hope of saving lives.

WHEN LIGHTNING STRIKES

All her life, June had a terrible fear of thunderstorms – a phobia, really. A clap of thunder would send her running into the nearest closet to hide. She would hang up the phone mid-sentence if she heard a rumble, fearing that lightning would strike her house and travel down the phone cord to reach her. Even her own adult children could not help her to overcome her paralysing fear.

When she retired, June moved into a sheltered apartment building. Her suite was on the top floor and had floor-to-ceiling windows. It seemed like a wonderful place – until the first storm. June felt exposed, with nowhere to hide in her new surroundings.

June's cat, Jeté, was a Devon rex, a breed known to be very vocal. The cat was rather neurotic (just like June) so June was used to hearing Jeté's lamentations for attention, demands to clean the litter box and other day-to-day chatter.

One day June heard her beloved cat calling from the bathroom. The litter box was kept there, so June assumed Jeté was unhappy with the state of the box and was calling her humble servant to clean it out. But just as June arrived in the bathroom to see what the fuss was about, there was a rumble of thunder and a flash of lightning. Jeté had called her into the one room in the apartment with no windows, just before the start of a thunderstorm.

June thought it was just a coincidence, until the next time there was a storm and Jeté again summoned her to the bathroom just before it began. It turned out that the cat was a very dependable predictor of storms, and June got in the habit of dashing for the bathroom when he called. The two of them would wait it out in the bathroom until the storm had passed.

June couldn't be sure whether the cat was also afraid of thunderstorms and hid in the bathroom for her own protection, or whether she understood that June was afraid and was calling her to protect her (or to avoid dealing with her panic). Either way, Jeté had learned to sense the atmospheric changes that precede a thunderstorm: changes in air pressure, or perhaps the electrical charge building in the air before a lightning strike. June was fortunate enough to have a cat that could keep her safely away from the windows before she felt exposed to the dangers, real or imagined, of a lightning bolt.

DID YOU KNOW?

On 26 December, 2004, a large earthquake near Indonesia set off a tsunami that moved through the Indian Ocean and struck land in several countries, killing over 150,000 people. Soon after the disaster, stories emerged of animals behaving strangely before the tsunami arrived, as though they knew it was coming.

Among the eyewitness accounts were stories about elephants in Sri Lanka running to higher ground, zoo animals hiding in their shelters, dogs refusing to go outside, flamingos leaving their coastal breeding areas and bats flying away. Some observers also expressed surprise at the low number of animal victims they found after the waters had receded. All of this led to speculation that the animals had predicted the tsunami.

Scientists have been mostly dismissive of the theories about tsunami-predicting animals. The stories are all anecdotal and there does not appear to be a consistent change in behaviour among all the animals in a given area. Some of the animal behaviours could simply have been coincidence. Others may provide insight into the more acute senses some animals possess. A tsunami will create low-frequency sounds as it approaches, which some animals can hear from very far away while they would be undetectable by humans. Just before the giant wave reached the shore, water would have been sucked out to sea from the shoreline; this could have caused a change in air pressure that some animals would notice.

It's impossible to say how many animals knew the tsunami was on the way, or how far in advance they could detect it. Could lives have been saved if local residents better understood animal behaviour? Perhaps the lesson is that if you live in a coastal area, and you see animals running for the hills, you should join them.

The Devon rex breed of cat is known for its intelligence and characteristically slender body, large ears and short hair.

A hotel on Phi Phi Island demolished by the tsunami in 2004.

PLAYING THE ODDS

Animals have been associated with gambling since ancient times. Roman chariot races were some of the first events to attract large-scale betting. Other events pitted animals against one another in fights to the death, with onlookers placing bets on which animal would survive. Betting on the outcome of contests between animals is alive and well today in thoroughbred horse and greyhound racing. Sadly, betting on vicious fights between animals, including roosters and dogs, still takes place too, although it is illegal in many countries.

But what about relying on animals to help you place your wagers on non-animal competitions? Would you trust an animal to predict the outcome of a soccer tournament, an Olympic event or even a political vote? While most people don't take animal predictions seriously, they are enormously popular – and it seems as if almost any kind of animal can be a prediction whiz.

A SPORTING CHANCE

One of the most popular events in the sporting world is the FIFA World Cup, which brings together soccer teams from around the globe. It's also an event that attracts a lot of gambling and predictions. While serious gamblers will look at a team's past performances and current players and try to make educated predictions based on the facts, other people are just looking to have a bit of fun with it.

Kleiner Paul (Little Paul), a successor to the original psychic octopus Paul, chooses the feeding box covered with the German flag instead of the Argentinian flag on 11 July, 2014, a few days ahead of the final match, Germany vs Argentina, at the FIFA World Cup.

Asking animals to predict the outcome of World Cup matches has become something of an obsession in several countries. The animal that brought this practice into the spotlight was Paul the octopus, who lived in a German aquarium. During the 2010 World Cup, Paul would be presented with two boxes, each containing food and each labelled with the flag of one of the teams competing in an upcoming match. Whichever box Paul ate from first was predicted to be the winner of the match. He correctly predicted the outcomes for six of Germany's matches in the tournament. He also correctly predicted the winner of the final between Spain and the Netherlands.

Paul did not live to see the next World Cup tournament in 2014, but many other animals in Germany were tried in his place, including Nelly the elephant, Norman the armadillo and an assortment of otters, penguins and even turtles. Other countries introduced their own animals to predict their teams' chances for victory. In Australia, a kangaroo was the natural choice. Flopsy the kangaroo proved unreliable but popular, with over 11,000 followers on Twitter during the tournament. The United Arab Emirates brought in a camel to help with their predictions. Shaheen the camel chose winning teams by touching his nose to one flag when presented with the two options. France's choice for a soccer-predicting mascot was somewhat unexpected: Watson the sea lion. He accurately predicted France's advancement to the quarter finals of the 2014 tournament.

POLITICAL BEASTS

People don't just bet on sporting events, though. You can bet on just about anything these days, and if you do you might want a bit of help from a prediction animal. You can even place a bet on the outcome of political events such as elections and referendums.

The 2016 Brexit referendum to determine whether the UK would leave the European Union was one of the biggest political events in Europe in recent years. Of course, British citizens had a say in the outcome by casting a vote, but there were all kinds of people and organizations making predictions about the outcome. There was also a goat.

Boots is a Golden Guernsey goat living in the town of Jedburgh, Scotland. Boots's owners dress him up in a tartan scarf and cap and let him make predictions of all kinds in front of visitors to their farm. Boots may look dapper, but his prediction methods are unsophisticated. He is taken to a display with two overturned flowerpots, each one with a sign on top. Boots makes his choice by choosing, or chewing, one of the signs. Boots correctly predicted the outcome of the Brexit vote, and has also weighed in on Scottish and international soccer matches.

The other major vote that took place in 2016 was the US presidential election. This was a story too big for just one animal! While many journalists and political commentators were surprised by the results of the election, several animals around the world seemed to have seen it coming.

In China, a monkey named Geda was presented with life-size cardboard cut-outs of the two presidential candidates, Hillary Clinton and Donald Trump. Geda chose to climb up on the Trump cut-out and give him a kiss, a clear sign of her preference.

Closer to the election action, dogs at a local dog park in Cleveland, Ohio were also asked to weigh in on the election. They were given the option of two toys to play with, one that looked like Clinton and the other like Trump. More of the dogs chose to chomp on the Trump toy, which was interpreted to mean that they preferred him.

Meanwhile in Florida, two university professors chose mako sharks as their substitutes for the candidates and had them compete in a race to the White House. Each shark had been tagged with a GPS locator to follow its movements in the Atlantic Ocean (presumably for research not related to the election) and the shark that had travelled the farthest by the Friday before the election was declared the winner. The Trump shark travelled over 1,050 kilometres (652 miles) while the Clinton shark only went 820 kilometres (510 miles).

At a park in Changsha, in China's Hunan province, Geda holds a fan with Chinese characters that read 'elected', before making his prediction on 3 November, 2016.

A SPRING THING

Winter weather can be unpredictable, but that doesn't stop people from betting on weather predictions, such as whether there will be snow on Christmas Day at a particular UK airport or whether the lowest or highest temperature record will be beaten in a certain year.

Perhaps the most famous weather prediction event is Groundhog Day in the United States, made more famous by the Bill Murray film of the same name. Groundhog Day, on 2 February, has a long history that dates back to the 19th century, and is based on even older superstitions. It is the date that falls halfway between the winter solstice (the shortest day of the year) and the spring equinox (when the day and night are of equal length). Ancient superstitions held that a bright, sunny day on that date meant the remaining part of the winter would be cold and stormy. Cloudy skies on 2 February, on the other hand, were said to predict that spring weather was just around the corner.

A group of groundhog hunters in the town of Punxsutawney, Pennsylvania started interpreting this old superstition with the help of a local groundhog. If the day was sunny, a groundhog emerging from his hole after the winter hibernation would see his shadow, get frightened by it, and run back inside. If the day was cloudy, there would be no shadow to see, so the groundhog would stay outside. In 1887, the local newspaper picked up the story of the Punxsutawney groundhog, named him Phil, and declared him to be America's official forecasting groundhog. The story eventually spread around the country, and while other towns and cities have selected their own local groundhogs to predict the coming of spring Punxsutawney Phil (who is replaced by a new generation as needed) is still the go-to groundhog for weather predictions.

So how optimistic is Phil when it comes to the arrival of spring? Looking at available statistics from 1887 through to 2015, he has been a pessimist overall. Phil has seen his shadow, predicting six more weeks of winter, 102 times in 127 years. Analysis of actual weather records from 1988 through to 2015 show that his predictions are not reliable (in case you were considering placing a large bet on his accuracy).

WE PREDICT CUTENESS!

Getting animals to predict the outcomes of sporting events is always fun and entertaining. But when it comes to being absolutely adorable, the clear winner of the prediction game is the Puppies Predict segment on the American nightly network staple *Late Night With Jimmy Fallon*. Using a group of seven puppies (to avoid a tie) and bowls of dog food labelled with the various teams or athlete names, winners are chosen depending on which bowl of food attracts the most puppies.

Punxsutawney Phil predicted an early spring at the 127th Groundhog Day Celebration at Gobbler's Knob on 2 February, 2013 in Punxsutawney, Pennsylvania. The Punxsutawney 'Inner Circle' claimed that there were about 35,000 people gathered at the event to watch Phil's annual forecast.

So far, the puppies have been called in to predict the outcomes of the Super Bowl, the World Series, the NCAA basketball playoffs and the Kentucky Derby, and they have ventured outside the sports world to predict the winner of Best Picture at the Academy Awards.

Bees have refined sensory abilities that allow them to determine where to find pollen from the colours of the flower.

The puppies may not always be right, but they are certainly always hungry! The show uses white golden retriever puppies from a North Carolina breeder, bringing in a new litter whenever the older pups have grown up and been moved to their permanent homes.

DID YOU KNOW?

Animals associate different colours and patterns with specific things such as food, danger and potential mates. When animals are asked to choose a sports team by picking a flag or a uniform, they may actually be basing their choice on the colours or patterns of the two choices.

For example, one of the theories behind the flag preferences shown by famous soccer predictor Paul the octopus was that he usually chose a flag with stripes over a flag without stripes. This would account for the fact that he chose Germany to win so many games. Many of the sea creatures that an octopus might enjoy eating also have stripes or contrasting colours, so an octopus could associate those visual cues with food.

Different animals perceive colours differently, including many species that can see colours in the ultraviolet spectrum that are invisible to humans. Birds and insects use this spectrum to identify flowers with pollen to collect.

Whatever the reasons for animals choosing certain colours or patterns over others, you can be sure that they aren't basing their choices on a sound knowledge of the sporting teams involved. If you're taking your advice from a four-legged source, or an eight-tentacled one for that matter, the odds are unlikely to be in your favour.

SELECTED BIBLIOGRAPHY

INTRODUCTION

Ancient Egypt Online, 'Ancient Egyptian Animals', www.ancient-egypt-online.com/ancient-egyptian-animals.html

Committee for Skeptical Inquiry, 'Superstition Bash: Spiders', www.csicop.org/superstition/library/spiders

Exemplore, 'Animal, Insect and Bird Omens and Meanings', http:// exemplore.com/spirit-animals/Omens-Oracles-And-Signs-Are-You-Superstitious

Government of Australia, 'The Dreaming', www.australia.gov.au/about-australia/australian-story/dreaming

Smith, William, 'Haruspices', in *A Dictionary of Greek and Roman Antiquities*, John Murray, London, 1875.

Tour Egypt, 'Animals and the Gods of Ancient Egypt', www.touregypt.net/featurestories/animalgods.htm

Witchcraft, 'Witchcraft Terms and Tools: Familiar', www.witchcraftandwitches.com/terms_familiar.html

ANIMAL GPS

Cats International, 'Incredible Journeys by Incredible Cats', catsinternational.org/incredible-journeys-by-incredible-cats/

Encyclopaedia Britannica, 'Migration, Animal: Navigation and Orientation', Encyclopaedia Britannica Online website, www.britannica.com/science/migration-animal/Navigation-and-orientation

H, Kathy, 'When Cats And Dogs Travel Long Distances To Get Home – Psi Trailing', Hub Pages website, 4 May, 2013, hubpages.com/animals/When-Cats-And-Dogs-Travel-Long-Distances-To-Get-Home-Psi-Trailing

Keeton, William T. and Klaus Schmidt-Koenig, eds, *Animal Migration, Navigation and Homing*, Springer Berlin Heidelberg, Berlin, 1978.

Know Your Cat, 'Kitty Come Home', http://www.knowyourcat.info/info/homing.htm

Macpherson, Krista and William A. Roberts, 'Spatial Memory in Dogs on a Radial Maze', *Journal of Comparative Psychology* 124:1, 47–56, 2010.

Miklosi, Adam, *Dog Behaviour, Evolution, and Cognition*, Oxford University Press, 2015.

Ministry of Natural Resources, Quebec, 'Caribou Migration Monitoring by Satellite Telemetry', mffp.gouv.qc.ca/english/wildlife/maps-caribou/index.jsp

Nature Journal, 'Humpback Whale Breaks Migration Record', www.nature.com/news/2010/101012/full/news.2010.532/slideshow/1.html?identifier=1

Robertson, Danielle, 'Homing Ability of Lost Cats', Lost Pet Research & Recovery website, http://lostpetresearch.com/2013/01/homing-ability-lost-cats/

Smithsonian Institution, 'Are Humans the Only Animals to Use the Stars To Navigate?', www.smithsonianmag.com/videos/category/ask-smithsonian/ask-smithsonian-are-humans-the-only-animals/

Stevick, Peter T., Mariana C. Neves, Freddy Johansen, Marcia H. Engel, Judith Allen, Milton C.C. Marcondes, Carole Carlson, 'A quarter of a world away: female humpback whale moves 10,000 km between breeding areas', *Biology Letters* 7:2, 23 April, 2011.

Urton, James, 'Scientists crack secrets of the monarch butterfly's internal compass', UW Today, University of Washington website, 14 April, 2016, www.washington.edu/news/2016/04/14/scientists-crack-secrets-of-the-monarch-butterflys-internal-compass/

Whale Facts, 'Whale Migration', www.whalefacts.org/why-do-whales-migrate/

ANIMALS TO THE RESCUE

Blumberg, Jess, 'A Brief History of the St. Bernard Rescue Dog', *Smithsonian Magazine* website, 1 March, 2016, www.smithsonianmag.com/history/a-brief-history-of-the-st-bernard-rescue-dog-13787665/

CARDA, 'News & Articles', Canadian Avalanche Rescue Dog Association website, www.carda.ca/pages/news-articles.php

Corday, Chris, 'Avalanche dog teams patrol ski resorts ready to save a life', CBC website, 26 December, 2016, www.cbc.ca/news/canada/british-columbia/avalanche-dog-team-ski-1.3907480

Gerritsen, Resi and Ruud Haak, *K9 Search and Rescue: A Manual for Training the Natural Way*, Dog Training Press, 2014.

Koenig, Marcia, 'The History of Search Dogs in the United States', Search and Rescue Assist website, 2009, www.searchandrescueassist.org/historyofsardogsUS.php

Maine Mounted Search and Rescue, 'Capabilities', www.mainemountedsar.org/capabilities

NZ USAR Search Dog Association, www.usardogs.org.nz/

Ohio Valley Search & Rescue Inc., 'Search Dog Training', www.vsar.org/SARdog.html

Rothwell, Jan, 'Tracking vs. Trailing', American Bloodhound Club website, www.americanbloodhoundclub.org/tracking-vs-trailing/

Truebridge, Nick, 'Christchurch Urban Search and Rescue responders look back at February 22', *The Press*, 22 February, 2016.

U.S. Department of Homeland Security, 'Canine's Role in Urban Search & Rescue', FEMA website, www.fema.gov/canines-role-urban-search-rescue

U.S. SAR Task Force, 'Dogs in Search and Rescue', www.ussartf.org/dogs_search_rescue.htm

Whirlwind Farms Inc., Equine Detection Services website, www.airscentinghorse.com/home.htm

COURAGE AND CAMARADERIE

American Racing Pigeon Union, 'Homing Pigeons Continue to Serve During Wartime', www.pigeon.org/pigeons_in_war6.htm

Dogs for Law Enforcement, 'Police Canines in History', www.dogsforlawenforcement.org/police-canines-in-history.html

Jackson, Amanda, 'Lucca the Marine dog receives medal for service', CNN website, 5 April, 2016, www.cnn.com/2016/04/05/us/lucca-marine-dog-medal-honor-irpt/

Moore, Malcolm, 'China trains army of messenger pigeons', *The Daily Telegraph*, 2 March, 2011.

Mott, Maryanne, 'Dogs of War: Inside the U.S. Military's Canine Corps', National Geographic News website, 9 April, 2003, news.nationalgeographic.com/news/2003/04/0409_030409_militarydogs.html

Parussini, Gabriele, 'In France, a Mission to Return the Military's Carrier Pigeons to Active Duty', *The Wall Street Journal*, 11 November, 2012.

Stromberg, Joseph, 'B.F. Skinner's Pigeon-Guided Rocket', *Smithsonian Magazine* website, 18 August, 2011, www.smithsonianmag.com/smithsonian-institution/bf-skinners-pigeon-guided-rocket-53443995/

United States War Dogs Association, www.uswardogs.org/

AT YOUR SERVICE

Assistance Dogs International, 'Types of Assistance Dogs', Assistance Dogs International website, www.assistancedogsinternational.org/about-us/types-of-assistance-dogs/

Dogs For Good, www.dogsforgood.org

International Association of Assistance Dog Partners, www.iaadp.org

Psychiatric Service Dog Partners, 'FAQ: Training – Basics', www.psychdogpartners.org/resources/frequently-asked-questions/faq-training-basics

U.S. Government Publishing Office, *Appendix A to Part 35—Guidance to Revisions to ADA Regulation on Nondiscrimination on the Basis of Disability in State and Local Government Services*, 15 September, 2010.

MEDICAL MARVELS

Chodosh, Sara, 'The Problem With Cancer-Sniffing Dogs', Popular Science website, 4 October, 2016, www.popsci.com/problem-with-cancer-sniffing-dogs

Dalziel, Deborah J., Basim M. Uthman, Susan P. McGorray and Roger L. Reep, 'Seizure-alert dogs: a review and preliminary study', *Seizure: European Journal of Epilepsy* 12:2, 115–20, March 2003.

Devereaux, Allison, 'Diabetes sniffing dogs studied by Dalhousie University researcher', CBC News website, 9 July, 2015, www.cbc.ca/news/canada/nova-scotia/diabetes-sniffing-dogs-studied-by-dalhousie-university-researcher-1.3143995

Gonder-Frederick, Linda, Pam Rice, Dan Warren, Karen Vajda and Jaclyn Shepard, 'Diabetic Alert Dogs: A Preliminary Survey of Current Users', *Diabetes Care*, April, 2013.

I F L Science, 'New Device Can Diagnose Diseases Just By Sniffing Your Breath', www.iflscience.com/technology/new-device-can-diagnose-diseases-just-sniffing-breath/

In Situ Foundation, 'Can Dogs Smell Cancer?' 1 September, 2015, dogsdetectcancer.org/can-dogs-smell-cancer/

Langley, Liz, 'How Dogs Can Sniff Out Diabetes and Cancer', National Geographic website, 19 March, 2016, news.nationalgeographic.com/2016/03/160319-dogs-diabetes-health-cancer-animals-science/

Lunenberg, T.C., 'Vibratory stimulation for the alleviation of chronic pain', *Acta Phisiologica Scandinavica Supplementum* 523, 1–51, 1983.

Marcus, Dawn, 'What can we learn from migraine alert dogs?' Migraine.com website, 13 January, 2011, migraine.com/blog/what-can-we-learn-from-migraine-alert-dogs/

Strong, Val, Stephen W. Brown and Robin Walker, 'Seizure-alert dogs – fact or fiction?' *Seizure: European Journal of Epilepsy* 8:1, 62–5, February 1999.

Webster, Rose, 'Do Cats Sense Human Illness?' Paw Mane Fin website, 7 June, 2014, www.pawmanefin.com/Do_Cats_Sense_Human_Illness

Welshman, Malcolm, 'Is your pet psychic? Animals can predict everything from natural disasters to sports results', *Mail Online*, 11 October, 2011, www.dailymail.co.uk/news/article-2047688/Animals-predict-natural-disasters-sports-results.html#ixzz4WDuviOVj

THERAPY ON FOUR LEGS

Dicker, Rachel, 'San Francisco Airport Introduces its First Therapy Pig', U.S. News & World Report website, 7 December, 2016, www.usnews.com/news/articles/2016-12-07/san-francisco-airport-introduces-its-first-therapy-pig

Equestrian Therapy, 'What Is Equestrian Therapy?', www.equestriantherapy.com/

Island Dolphin Care, www.islanddolphincare.org/

Morry, Melina, 'Therapy Dogs In Canadian Airports: Get Licked And Love It', *Vane Magazine* website, 17 March, 2016, www.magazine.vaneairport.com/play/therapy-dogs/therapy-dogs-in-canadian-airports/

Oksman, Olga, 'Paws for Thought: How Pet Therapy is Gaining Traction', *The Guardian* website, December 30, 2015, www.theguardian.com/lifeandstyle/2015/dec/30/animal-assisted-therapy-nih-veterinary-science-mental-health-american-heart-association

Owen, Erika, 'Meet America's Completely Adorable Airport Therapy Dogs', Travel + Leisure website, www.travelandleisure.com/articles/airport-therapy-dogs

Petergreenberg.com, 'Travel Tip: Where You Can Find Therapy Dogs at Airports', 4 June, 2015, petergreenberg.com/2015/06/04/therapy-dogs-at-airports/

Pets as Therapy, 'What We Do', petsastherapy.org/what-we-do/

Temple University, 'Science of Therapy Dogs', 9 December, 2013, library.temple.edu/node/39122

Therapy Dogs International, www.tdi-dog.org

Wang, Shirley S., 'Rise in Pets as Therapy for Mental Conditions', *The Wall Street Journal*, 4 November, 2013.

Weaver, Jane, 'Puppy love – it's better than you think', NBC News website, 8 April, 2004, www.nbcnews.com/id/4625213/ns/health-pet_health/t/puppy-love----its-better-you-think/#. WIDpdxsrJPa

ARE YOU MY MOTHER?

Celizic, Mike, 'Tigers say "Bye, mom" to dog that raised them', Today website, 25 June, 2009, www.today.com/news/tigers-say-bye-mom-dog-raised-them-wbna31541834

Dell'Amore, Christine, 'Why Animals "Adopt" Others, Including Different Species', National Geographic News website, 12 May, 2013, news.nationalgeographic.com/news/2013/04/130510-adoption-deformed-dolphin-reddit-science-animals-weird/

Di Jensen, Elle, 'Dogs Raising Kittens', The Nest website, pets.thenest.com/dogs-raising-kittens-4693.html

Frison, Megan, 'Why do animals adopt?' Ian Somerhalder Foundation website, www.isfoundation.com/news/why-do-animals-adopt

Goldman, Jason G., 'Why Do Animals Adopt?' BBC Future website, 12 March, 2014, www.bbc.com/future/story/20140312-why-do-animals-adopt

Hartman, Steve, 'Mother of the Year? Dog Nurses Kittens', CBS News website, 9 May, 2008, www.cbsnews.com/news/mother-of-the-year-dog-nurses-kittens/

Hoffman, Piper, '4 Mother Animals Who Adopted Babies of Different Species', Care2 website, 9 October, 2012, www.care2.com/causes/5-mama-animals-adopt-babies-of-different-species.html

Lingle, Susan and Tobias Riede, 'Deer Mothers Are Sensitive to Infant Distress Vocalizations of Diverse Mammalian Species', *The American Naturalist* 184:4, 510–22, October 2014.

Mueller, Corsin A. and Matthew B.V. Bell, 'Kidnapping and infanticide between groups of banded mongooses', *Mammalian Biology* 74:4, 315–8, 2009.

Nsubuga, Jimmy, 'Dog adopts orphaned piglets after their mum dies', Metro UK website, 4 September, 2016, metro.co.uk/2016/09/04/dog-adopts-orphaned-piglets-after-their-mum-dies-6108476/#ixzz4WESX6LSY

Riehl, Christina, 'Evolutionary routes to non-kin cooperative breeding in birds', *Proceedings of the Royal Society* 280:1772, December 7, 2013.

Rogak, Lisa, *One Big Happy Family*, St. Martin's Griffin, New York, 2013.

Science Blogs, 'Adoption in Non-Human Primates', The Primate Diaries, 17 July, 2009, scienceblogs.com/primatediaries/2009/07/17/adoption-in-non-human-primates/

Stallard, Brian, 'Cross Species Baby Love: Confusion or Compassion?' Nature World News website, 18 September, 2014, www.natureworldnews.com/articles/9099/20140918/cross-species-baby-love-confusion-compassion.htm

Young, Ann, 'A long tailed macaque monkey adopts a kitten in the forests of Bali, Indonesia', the *Telegraph* website, www.telegraph.co.uk/news/earth/earthpicturegalleries/7963657/A-long-tailed-macaque-monkey-adopts-a-kitten-in-the-forests-of-Bali-Indonesia.html

FURRY FORECASTERS

Donaldson-Evans, Catherine, 'Tsunami Animals: A Sixth Sense?' Fox News website, 9 January,

2005, www.foxnews.com/story/2005/01/09/tsunami-animals-sixth-sense.html

Highfield, Roger, 'Did they sense the tsunami?' the *Telegraph* website, 8 January, 2005, www.telegraph.co.uk/technology/3337851/Did-they-sense-the-tsunami.html

Kirschvink, Joseph L., 'Earthquake Prediction by Animals: Evolution and Sensory Perception', *Bulletin of the Seismological Society of America* 90:2, 213–23, April 2000.

Mott, Maryanne, 'Did Animals Sense Tsunami Was Coming?' National Geographic News website, 5 January, 2005, news.nationalgeographic.com/news/2005/01/0104_050104_tsunami_animals.html

PBS, 'Can Animals Predict Disaster?' Nature website, 3 June, 2008, www.pbs.org/wnet/nature/can-animals-predict-disaster-tall-tales-or-true/131/

RT, 'Animal instincts: Chinese city uses dogs to predict quakes', RT News website, 7 May, 2013, www.rt.com/news/chinese-dogs-predict-earthquakes-946/

Schaal, Rand B., 'An Evaluation of the Animal-Behavior Theory for Earthquake Prediction', *California Geology*, 41–5, 1988.

U.S. Geological Survey, 'Animals & Earthquake Prediction', USGS website, earthquake.usgs.gov/learn/topics/animal_eqs.php

PLAYING THE ODDS

Battaglia, Chris, 'Animals vs. Machines: What is better at predicting World Cup results?' The Score website, 3 July, 2014, www.thescore.com/news/532028

Deninno, Nadine, 'An Octopus Made Better World Cup Predictions Than Goldman Sachs', International Business Times website, 27 June, 2014, www.ibtimes.com/octopus-made-better-world-cup-predictions-goldman-sachs-photos-1613882

Moye, David, 'Psychic Animals Favor Trump in the Election', the *Huffington Post* website,

7 November, 2016, www.huffingtonpost.com/entry/psychic-animals-election-predicitons_us_5820b4fbe4b0e80b02cb7e04

National Oceanic and Atmospheric Association, 'Groundhog Day', National Centers for Environmental Information website, www.ncdc.noaa.gov/customer-support/education-resources/groundhog-day

Online Casino Reports, 'Placing Odds on Groundhog Day', 31 January, 2006, www.onlinecasinoreports.com/articles/placing-odds-on-groundhog-day.php

Pagan, Katy, 'Boots the psychic goat predicts gruff times for England at Euro 2016', The Scottish Sun website, 11 June, 2016, www.thescottishsun.co.uk/archives/football/160183/boots-the-psychic-goat-predicts-gruff-times-for-england-at-euro-2016/

Recherche Goldens, 'Available Pups', whitegoldenretriever.com

ACKNOWLEDGEMENTS

Writing a book is never as solitary a task as it sounds, so I would like to take this opportunity to thank everyone who shared their time, expertise and experiences with me. First, thanks to Arcturus Publishing and Daniel Conway who gave me the perfect excuse to explore two of my passions: science and animals. I am also grateful to those who answered my call with their amazing stories, including Alex Anderson, Rob Clayton, Hollie Devlin, April Hubbard, Anne Kennedy, Laurie Ann March, Nicole McKechnie, Margriet Ruurs, Jordan Sharp, Sean Thrush, Des Moines County Humane Society and NZ USAR Search Dog Association. Finally, I'd like to thank my wonderful husband, Gerhard, for all his love and support, and our two beautiful (but not psychic) dogs, Marlowe and Nuka, who remind me to live in the moment and laugh every day.

INDEX